KS2
Success
SATs

Science

Jackie Clegg

Contents

Plants

Animals and ecosystems

Humans

Materials

Physical processes

Science investigations

Notes

Answers

Flowering plants

The structure of the flowering plant

The flowering plant is made up of different parts. Each part of the plant has its own job to do.

The **roots** anchor the plant into the ground and take in water from the soil.
The **leaves** are where food is made for the plant.
The **stem** carries food and water to the different parts of the plant.
The **flower** is where reproduction takes place.

SATs practice

LEVEL 3 The diagram shows a plant. Label the diagram. Choose your words from this list.

flower   leaf   root

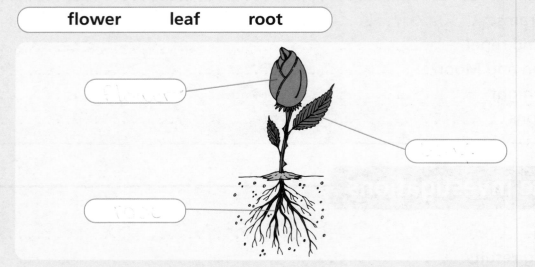

LEVEL 4 This table shows the jobs of the different parts of the plant. Finish the table by writing the part of the plant next to the job it does. The first one has been done for you.

part of plant	the job it does
stem	Carries food and water to different parts of the plant.
leaves	Where food is made for the plant.
roots	Anchors the plant into the ground.
flower	Where reproduction takes place.

a Tim is planting some young plants in his garden. The instructions say "plant 30 cm apart". Explain why the young plants need so much space between them.

_____

b Tim pulls the leaves off one plant. Explain why a plant without leaves will not grow as well as the other plants.

_____

Inside the flower

The flower is made up of different parts. Each part has its own job to do.
The **stamen** is the male part of the flower, where pollen is made and stored.
The **stigma** has a sticky surface to catch pollen.
The **style** is where the pollen passes through to reach the female ovum.
The **petals** are brightly coloured and scented to attract insects.
The **sepal** protects the flower whilst it is developing inside the bud.

SATs practice

 The diagram shows the structure of a flower. Label the diagram. Choose your words from this list.

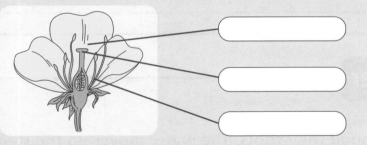

petal

sepal

stamen

stigma

style

 Finish these sentences by filling in the missing words. Choose your words from this list.

| flower | petal | sepal | stamen | stigma | style |

Reproduction takes place in the _____. When the flower is in bud, it is protected by the _____. Pollen lands on the sticky _____. Pollen is made and stored in the _____.

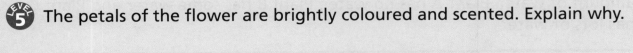 The petals of the flower are brightly coloured and scented. Explain why.

_____

What plants need to grow

Photosynthesis

Plants make their own food by a process called **photosynthesis**.

For photosynthesis to take place, plants need light and water.

Most photosynthesis takes place in the **leaves**.

SATs practice

For plants to grow, they need two important things.

LEVEL 3 Circle the two things needed by plants for growth.

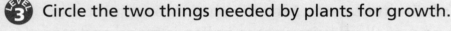

fibre   water   vitamins   light

LEVEL 4 Circle the process by which plants make their own food.

germination   photosynthesis   pollination

LEVEL 5 Sunflower plants turn to face the sun. Explain why plants turn to face the Sun.

_____

Plants need water

Plants take in water through their roots. The water moves up the stem of the plant to the leaves. In the leaves the water is then used in photosynthesis to make food for the plant. A plant without water will start to wilt and die.

SATs practice

Becky is investigating how plants grow. She has three identical plants. She puts them all in the same window. Becky waters each plant with a different amount of water. Plant A has no water, Plant B has some water and Plant C has lots of water.

Becky is investigating one factor for growth. Circle the factor Becky is investigating.

air   light   water   pollination

 Describe one thing Becky must do to make this a fair test.

_____

 Which plant will grow best?   Plant _____

Give a reason for your choice.

_____

_____

Plants need light

Plants need **light energy** for photosynthesis to take place. A green chemical called **chlorophyll** absorbs light. Plants that are left in the dark start to turn yellow and will eventually die.

SATs practice

 What do all plants need to grow well? Tick **two** boxes.

soil ☐   water ☐   worms ☐   light ☐

 These plants are growing in different places. Draw a straight line to match the plants with the description of where they are growing.

a dry place with very little water   a dark shady place with very little light and water   a place with lots of sunlight and water

 Emma is growing plants in her garden. The plants under the tree are not growing as well as the plants in the centre of the lawn. Explain why.

_____

How plants reproduce

Pollination

When plants grow, they produce flowers. The flower contains the reproductive organs of the plant.

Pollen is the male cell of the plant. It needs to reach the female cell. The female cells are in the **ovary**.

Pollen is stored in the **anther**. The pollen is moved from the anther of one flower to the stigma of another flower. The pollen is carried by **insects** or by **wind**.

SATs practice

The picture shows a flowering plant.

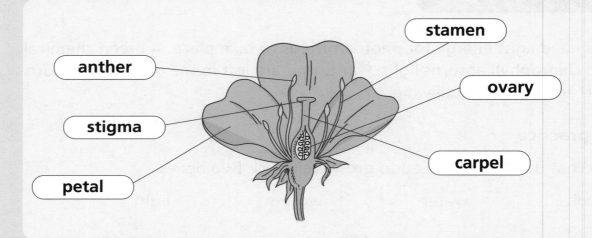

On the picture, circle the part where pollen is stored.

This plant is pollinated by insects. Write down the other method by which pollination can take place.

_____

Explain one way in which this plant is adapted for **insect pollination**.

_____

_____

Different methods of seed dispersal

ANIMAL DISPERSAL
Some seeds grow hooks that grip to the fur or feathers of animals. Other seeds are inside fruits and are eaten by animals.

WIND DISPERSAL
Some seeds have wings or parachutes that help them travel in the wind.

EXPLOSION DISPERSAL
When the seed pods dry out, they curl back and shoot seeds into the air.

WATER DISPERSAL
Seeds drop from the plant, then float across the water.

SATs practice

The picture shows some berries that contain seeds.

LEVEL 3 What is the type of dispersal for the seeds in these berries? Circle the correct type of seed dispersal.

> animal dispersal   explosion dispersal   wind dispersal

LEVEL 4 Tick one box to show how birds help to disperse these seeds.

The seeds grip onto the feathers. ☐

Birds spread seeds in their droppings. ☐

Birds shake the seeds out of the berries. ☐

LEVEL 5 One plant will produce many seeds. Explain why plants need to produce many seeds.

_____

_____

Life cycle of plants

Germination

Germination is the start of the plant's **life cycle**.
Germination is the stage when seeds start to grow.
For germination to take place, seeds need air, warmth and moisture.

SATs practice

Tom and Molly are investigating what seeds need for germination to take place.
Tom puts cotton wool in three dishes. Molly puts ten cress seeds in each dish.

Tom puts one dish in the refrigerator, one in a box in the garden and the other in a dark cupboard in the classroom. Molly waters them each day.

 Tom and Molly are carrying out a fair test. Write down one factor they keep the same.

_____

The table shows their results.

place	number of seeds germinated		
	day 1	day 2	day 3
refrigerator	0	0	0
garden	0	1	6
classroom	0	5	10

Circle the factor Molly and Tom are investigating.

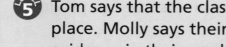

amount of air   amount of water   temperature

 Tom says that the classroom is the best place for germination to take place. Molly says their results support his conclusion. Explain how the evidence in their results table supports their conclusion.

_____

_____

Life cycle

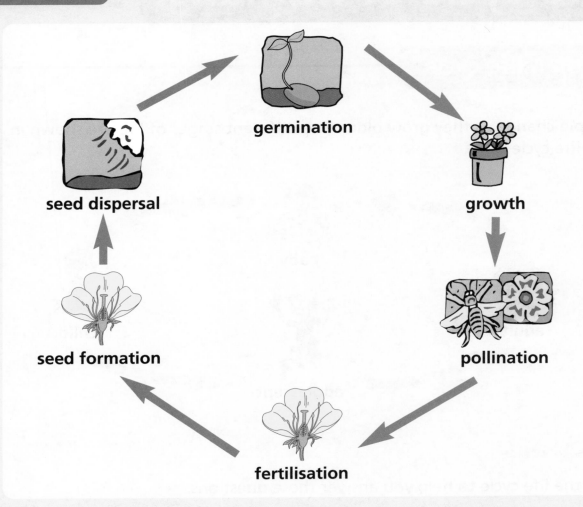

germination

growth

pollination

fertilisation

seed formation

seed dispersal

SATs practice

 Circle the word that describes when seeds start to grow.

> fertilisation   germination   growth

LEVEL 4 Write down the part of the plant where the seeds form.

_____

LEVEL 5 Pollen grains move from the anther of one flower to the stigma of another flower. Describe how pollen grains move from flower to flower.

_____

_____

Life cycle of humans

Human life cycle

People change as they grow older. The different stages of life are shown in this life cycle.

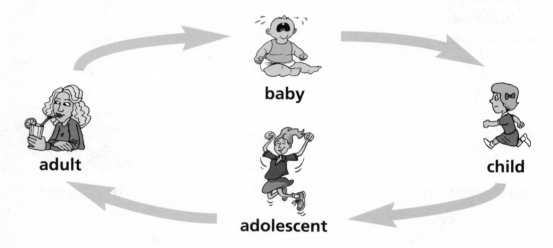

baby

child

adolescent

adult

SATs practice

Use the life cycle to help you answer these questions.

3 Finish the time line.

baby ⟶ child ⟶ adolescent ⟶ _____

4 At what stage is the human most dependent on their parents?

_____

5 At what age is **adolescence**? Circle the correct answer.

| 0 – 2 years | 5 – 8 years | 12 – 18 years | 50 – 60 years |

Metamorphosis

Some animals change completely during their life. This is called **metamorphosis**.

The different stages of metamorphosis are shown in this life cycle of a ladybird.

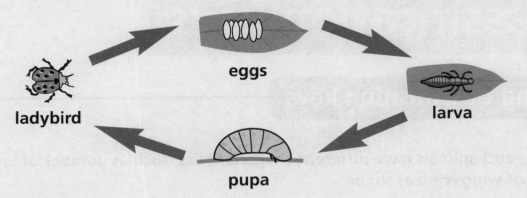

SATs practice

Use the life cycle to help you answer these questions.

3 Finish the time line.

eggs ⟶ larva ⟶ _____ ⟶ ladybird

4 What is the name given to the adult insect in this life cycle?

_____

5 Ladybirds eat greenfly and their larvae eat leaves. Suggest an advantage to the difference in food supply at various stages of the life cycle.

_____

The importance of reproduction

Reproduction is important because it means that more animals and plants can grow. Some animals and plants are becoming **extinct**. Conservationists and zoos are helping to prevent some animals and plants from dying out.

SATs practice

3 Circle the place where animals are kept to stop them dying out.

    pond   hospital   zoo

4 Circle the animal that is in danger of becoming extinct.

    cat   dog   panda   horse

5 Explain what is meant by the word **extinct**.

_____

Classification keys

Using classification keys

Plants and animals have different **characteristics**, such as number of legs, pairs of wings or leaf shape.

Things can be sorted into groups according to their characteristics. **Classification keys** can be used to identify plants and animals. Each part of the key asks a question about their characteristics.

SATs practice

A  B  C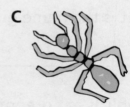

LEVEL 3 Use the key to identify these small animals.

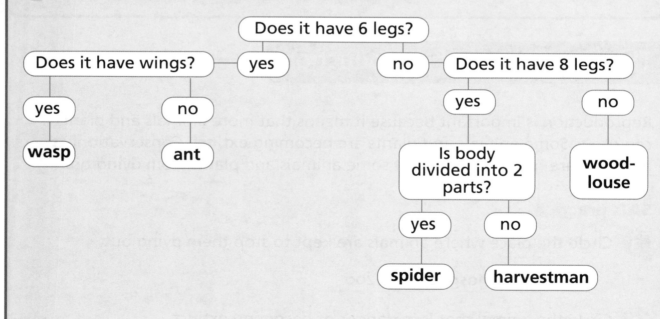

A = _____

B = _____

C = _____

Use the key to help you answer these questions.

LEVEL 4 Does a woodlouse have 8 legs? _____

LEVEL 5 Write down **two** facts about harvestmen.

1 _____

2 _____

Venn diagrams

Another way to sort plants and animals is to use Venn diagrams.

Plants and animals that share the same characteristics are placed in the overlapping parts of the circles.

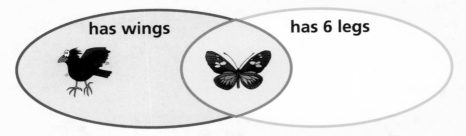

has wings   has 6 legs

SATs practice

Use the Venn diagram to help you answer these questions.

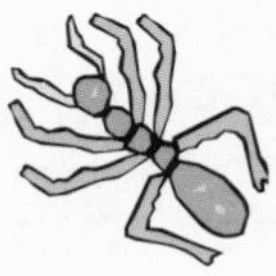

A    B    C

LEVEL 3 **On the diagram** write **A**, **B** and **C**, to show where each animal belongs.

LEVEL 4 Explain why you put animal **A** into that group on the diagram.

_____

LEVEL 5 Write down the **two** features of the animals in the centre of the Venn diagram.

1 _____

2 _____

Processes of life

The seven processes of life

All living things (plants and animals) carry out seven life processes:

- Feeding
- Moving
- Feeling
- Breathing
- Waste
- Growing
- Babies

All living things produce waste.

All living things produce young.

SATs practice

Look at the pictures.

boy

teddy

plant

 3 The first picture shows the boy eating. This is one of the seven processes of life. Circle **one other** life process.

> breathing   evaporating   floating

 4 Write down one of the processes the teddy cannot do.

_____

5 The plant is living. Name the process of feeding carried out by plants.

_____

_____

Is it alive?

Living things carry out **all seven** processes of life.

This is sometimes difficult to see in plants.

Plants make their own food (Feeding). Plants move to face sunlight. They take in air (Breathe) and give out air (Waste). You can see them grow and produce seeds (Babies). Although plants do not have feelings, they do respond to light and gravity; this is the plant's way of feeling.

SATs practice

Look at the pictures.

| human | toy soldier | plant |

3 The human and the plant are living things. Circle **one** of the life processes that is carried out by living things.

> dissolving   growing   rusting

4 Write down the life process shown by both the human and the toy soldier.

_____

5 The toy soldier is showing one of the living processes of life. Explain why the toy soldier is not a living thing.

_____

_____

Harmful micro-organisms

What is a micro-organism?

Micro means tiny. Organism means a complete living thing.
So **micro-organism** means a tiny living thing.
Micro-organisms show all seven life processes.
You need a microscope to look at micro-organisms.
Micro-organisms include **bacteria**, **viruses** and **fungi**.
Do not use the word 'germs'. Try to be more scientific and use the key words.

SATs practice

Sayed is investigating mouldy bread. He puts identical slices of bread into plastic bags. He places the bags in different places in the kitchen. After five days, Sayed looks at his results, which are shown in the diagram.

window sill	kitchen table	fridge	freezer
lots of mould	some mould	very little mould	no mould

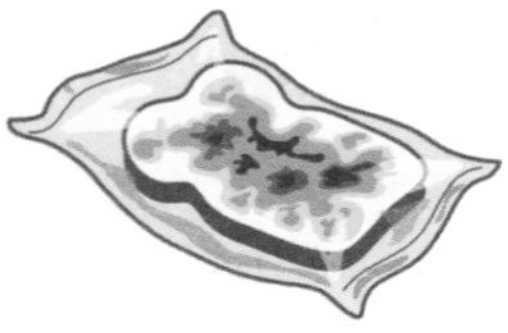

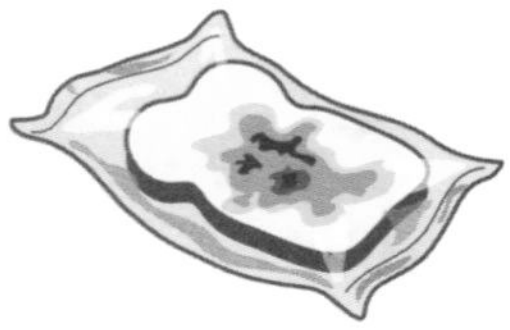

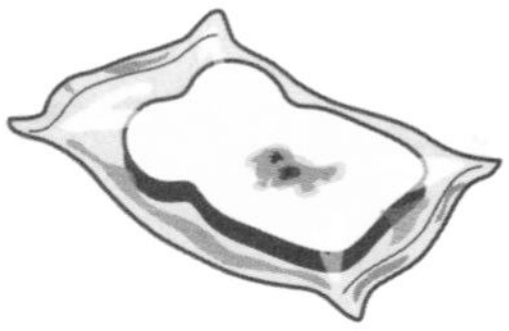

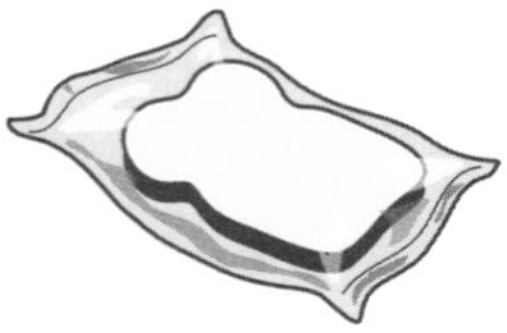

3 What factor about growth of mould is Sayed investigating? Circle the correct answer.

size of bread   temperature   time left

4 Sayed wants to make this a fair test. Write down **one** factor Sayed keeps the same to make this a fair test.

_____

5 Write a conclusion for this investigation. Describe how temperature affects the growth of mould on bread.

_____

_____

Harmful micro-organisms

Some micro-organisms can make us ill.
Some micro-organisms cause food to decay.

Illnesses caused by **viruses** include flu, measles and mumps.

Illnesses caused by **bacteria** include stomach upsets, food poisoning and ear infections.

The mould on bread are an example of **fungi**. Fungi can also cause athlete's foot.

The picture shows some foods found in a kitchen.

SATs practice

 What should be prevented from entering the packet of bacon, in order to stop micro-organisms growing? Circle the correct answer.

air   warmth   water

 Explain how freezing helps to preserve the fish fingers.

_____

_____

 Before food is put into cans, it is heated to a high temperature. Explain how this process helps to preserve food.

_____

_____

Helpful micro-organisms

What micro-organisms need to grow

Micro-organisms are living things. They need air, warmth and water to grow and reproduce. Without any of these factors, micro-organisms cannot live.

SATs practice

Alexander Fleming was a scientist who lived a long time ago. He discovered a useful mould called penicillin.

Alexander Fleming was growing bacteria in dishes. Some of the special mould landed in the dishes by accident. A few days later, Fleming noticed that the bacteria around the mould had started to die. Penicillin is still used today to treat bacterial infections.

LEVEL 3 Circle the word that describes when someone notices something.

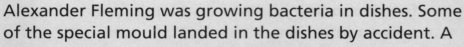

conclusion   observation   prediction

LEVEL 4 What **three** things did the mould need to grow? Tick the correct boxes.

air ☐   warmth ☐   light ☐

water ☐   dark ☐   fire ☐

LEVEL 5 What caused the bacteria to die?

_____

Micro-organisms in food production

Bacteria are used to make yoghurt and cheese. Yeast is used to make bread, beer and wine.

SATs practice

Kerry carried out an investigation to see how yeast makes bread rise. In each tub she put the same amount of flour, yeast and warm water. She placed each tub in a different place in the kitchen and left them for two hours.

The table shows her results.

kitchen table	fridge	warm cupboard
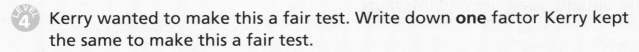		
height bread has risen 3 cm	height bread has risen 0 cm	height bread has risen 12 cm

 LEVEL 3 What factor was Kerry investigating? Circle the correct word.

> air   temperature   water

LEVEL 4 Kerry wanted to make this a fair test. Write down **one** factor Kerry kept the same to make this a fair test.

_____

LEVEL 5 Write a conclusion for this investigation. Describe how temperature affects the growth of yeast.

_____

Micro-organisms and decay

Micro-organisms cause some materials to decay by eating them.
It is helpful that micro-organisms break down dead plants and animals.

SATs practice

LEVEL 3 Not all materials can be broken down. Tick **two** boxes to show materials that **cannot** be broken down.

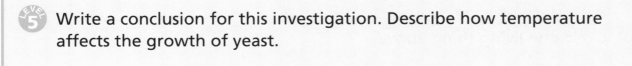
plastic bags ☐   glass bottles ☐   bread ☐   apples ☐

LEVEL 4 Describe **how** micro-organisms break down materials.

_____

LEVEL 5 Explain why it is **helpful** for micro-organisms to break down dead plants and animals.

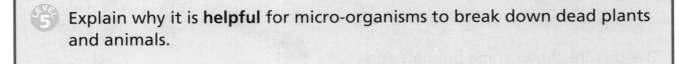
_____

Habitats

What is a habitat?

A **habitat** is a place where plants and animals live.

A **community** is all the living things in a habitat.

An **ecosystem** is a habitat and its community.

Examples of habitats include: desert, polar ice caps, rivers, jungles, gardens, mountains, seashore and lots more.

SATs practice

Sarah is investigating her garden.
The pictures show some things Sarah can see.

 Circle **one** living thing above.

 The **place** where all of these things live is called a…
Circle the correct word.

community	ecosystem	habitat

 Write down the things in the picture that form a **community**.

_____

Animals in their habitat

Each animal is suited to its habitat. A fish could not survive living in a sandy desert and a camel could not live in the sea. Animals depend upon their habitat for food, shelter and somewhere to hide.

SATs practice

The picture shows some animals and some habitats.

LEVEL 3 Draw **three** lines to match each animal to its habitat.

LEVEL 4 Write down **one other** thing that would form part of a community in the pond.

____

LEVEL 5 Explain how the tadpole is suited to its habitat.

____

____

Plants in their habitat

Plants are also suited to their habitat. Cactus plants grow well in the desert and seaweed grows well in the sea. Plants depend upon their habitat for sunlight, water, anchorage and air. Farmers and gardeners add fertilisers to the soil to help plants to grow big and healthy.

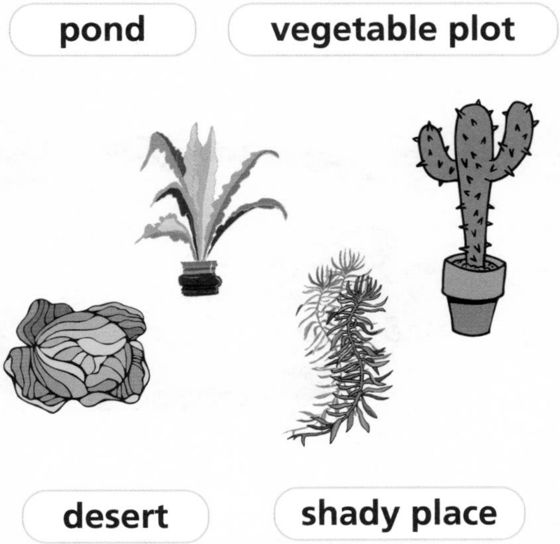
pond
vegetable plot
desert
shady place

SATs practice

The picture shows some plants.

LEVEL 3 Draw **four** lines to match each plant to its habitat.

LEVEL 4 The gardener put fertiliser onto the vegetable plot. Explain why.

____

LEVEL 5 One of the plants has pale leaves and is growing long and spindly. Explain why the habitat for this plant has caused this type of growth.

____

____

Food chains

Producers

Food chains show how energy moves from one organism to another.

At the start of all food chains are plants.

Plants are called **producers**, because they produce their own food.

Plants need **energy** from **sunlight** to make their food.

Plants make their own food by a process called **photosynthesis**.

This food energy is then passed through the food chain.

SATs practice

The picture shows the life cycle of a ladybird.

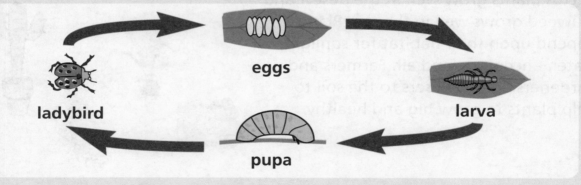

Level 3 The producer in this picture is the... Circle the correct word.

egg   plant   ladybird

Level 4 Where does the producer get its energy from?

_____

Level 5 Give **two** reasons why the plant is important to the life cycle of a ladybird.

1 _____

2 _____

Food chains show feeding relationships

Producers are eaten by **primary consumers**.

Primary consumers are eaten by **secondary consumers**.

The consumer at the end of the food chain can also be called the **tertiary consumer**.

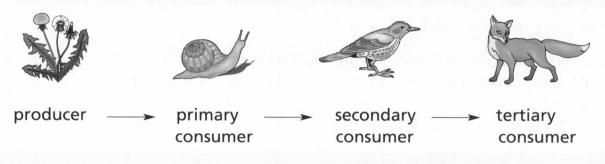

producer → primary consumer → secondary consumer → tertiary consumer

The line → means 'is eaten by'.

Animals that eat plants are called **herbivores**.
Animals that eat other animals are called **carnivores**.

SATs practice

The diagram shows a food chain.

corn   **mouse**   **owl**

3 One of the living things in this food chain is a **producer**. Tick the correct box to show which is the producer.

corn ☐

mouse ☐

owl ☐

4 Write down the name of the **herbivore** in this food chain.

_____

5 Write down the key word that describes the **owl** in this food chain.

_____

Food webs

Lots of food chains

Herbivores eat more than one type of plant and most **carnivores** eat more than one type of animal.

This means that food chains become linked together.
When food chains become connected, it is called a **food web**.

SATs practice

The picture shows a food web.

3 On the diagram, draw a circle around the **producers**.

4 What is the **tertiary consumer** in this food web?

_____

5 Explain how energy passes through the food web.

_____

_____

Changes to food webs

All parts of the food web are connected. Sometimes one part of the food web can change.

For example, the rabbits might catch a disease and die. This means the fox will need to eat more birds.

SATs practice

Look at the food web on the opposite page.

3 The gardener removes all of the lettuces from his garden. Which **two** animals will have less food to eat? Tick the **two** correct boxes.

dandelions	☐	snail	☐
rabbit	☐	bird	☐
fox	☐	cat	☐

4 Describe what will happen to the rabbits and snails if all of the lettuces are removed from the garden.

_____

_____

5 Describe **one other** effect on the food chain when all of the lettuces are removed.

_____

_____

Animals are adapted to their environment

Penguins

To adapt means to change. Animals adapt to their **environment**.

Penguins could not survive in the desert.
Penguins are adapted for life in a cold environment.

To survive in the cold, penguins have:
- soft, fluffy feathers close to their body to keep heat in
- waterproof feathers on the surface
- streamlined body to help them swim.

SATs practice

These animals live in different environments.

animal	climate	one way this animal has adapted to its environment	how this adaptation helps it to survive
 _____	cold		
 _____	mild	Reddish-brown fur	camouflage, so prey cannot see its approach

3 In the table, write the names of the animals under their pictures.

4 In the table, describe one adaptation.

5 Explain how this adaptation helps the animal to survive in its environment.

_____

_____

Camels

A desert is a hot, dry environment. Camels are adapted for life in desert conditions.

To survive in the desert, camels have:

- a store of food and water in the fleshy hump on their back
- leathery eyelids to protect their eyes from the glare of the Sun
- long eyelashes to keep sand out of their eyes
- flat, wide feet to stop them sinking into the sand.

SATs practice

The picture shows two living things that are adapted for life in the desert.

 **camel**    **cactus**

3 The camel is adapted to live in the desert. Tick **two** boxes that describe adaptations of the camel.

fluffy feathers	☐	leathery eyelids	☐
flat, wide feet	☐	long tail	☐
streamlined body	☐	large wings	☐

4 Camels can survive for two weeks without water. Explain how camels are adapted to cope without water.

_____

_____

5 The cactus plant is adapted to live in hot, dry conditions. Name one adaptation of the cactus plant and explain how this adaptation helps it to survive.

adaptation _____

explanation _____

_____

The heart and the circulatory system

The heart

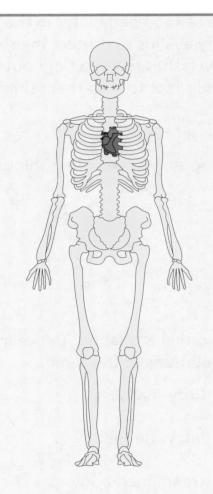

Blood is moving around your body all the time. Your **heart** pumps the blood around your body. The muscle walls of the heart squeeze together to force blood out of the heart and around the body.

Your heart is about the size of your clenched fist. It is positioned in your chest, between your lungs. Your heart is protected by your ribcage.

SATs practice

We need blood to stay alive.

 Which organ pumps blood around the body? Circle the correct answer.

> brain   heart   lungs

 The heart is protected by the skeleton. Which part of the skeleton protects the heart?

_____

 Describe how the heart forces blood around the body.

_____

_____

Blood vessels

Blood vessels carry blood all around the body.
The blood vessels that take blood away from the heart are called **arteries**.
The blood vessels that take blood back to the heart are called **veins**.

SATs practice

The heart pumps blood around the body.

 On the diagram, draw a circle to show the position of the heart.

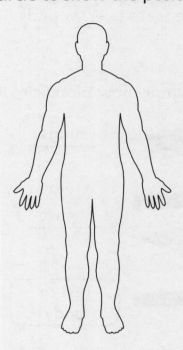

 How is blood carried around the body? Tick **two** correct boxes.

Blood is carried away from the heart in veins. ☐

Blood is carried away from the heart in arteries. ☐

Blood is carried around the body in special pipes. ☐

Blood is carried back to the heart in veins. ☐

Blood is carried back to the heart in arteries. ☐

 If someone cuts open an artery, blood spurts from the wound and it is difficult to stop the bleeding. Explain why.

_____

_____

Blood

What does blood do?

Your blood is a liquid made up of different types of cells.
It has many jobs to do around the body:
- to carry oxygen and food to all body cells
- to carry waste products away from all body cells
- to fight disease by destroying micro-organisms
- to clot together to form scabs over wounds.

SATs practice

The diagram shows very simply how blood circulates the body.

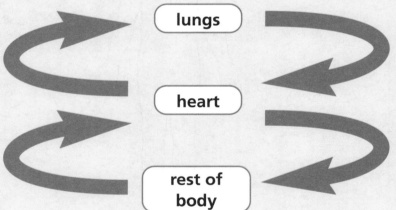

LEVEL 3 Blood moves from the lungs to the… Circle the correct answer.

    heart   lungs   rest of body

LEVEL 4 The blood collects a gas from the lungs. This important gas is…
Tick the correct box.

carbon dioxide   ☐

hydrogen   ☐

oxygen   ☐

LEVEL 5 Blood carries food and oxygen to all the cells in the body. Explain why.

_____

_____

Pulse rates

Every time your heart beats, it pumps blood around the body. As blood is pumped, it causes a ripple through your arteries. Where arteries are close to the surface of your skin, you can feel this ripple. It is called your **pulse**. Your **pulse rate** is the number of beats (or ripples) per minute.

When you exercise, your muscles need more energy. To provide the energy, your muscle cells need more oxygen and food, so your heart has to beat faster to move more oxygen and food around your body. This causes your pulse rate to increase.

SATs practice

Jane is going to run in a race. She takes her pulse before the race.

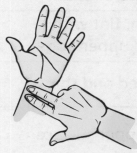

3 (LEVEL) What does pulse rate measure? Tick the correct box.

how fast your blood is flowing ☐

how fast your heart is beating ☐

how fast you are breathing ☐

4 (LEVEL) After the race, Jane sits down and rests for 10 minutes. Predict what happened to Jane's pulse rate during the 10 minutes.

_____

_____

5 (LEVEL) Jane took her pulse at the end of the race. Jane's pulse rate had increased. Explain why pulse rate increases during exercise.

_____

_____

Teeth

Types of teeth and their job

Some animals use teeth for defence. All animals use teeth for eating food. Different animals eat different foods and this means different types of teeth.

A 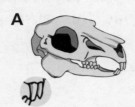 **B**  **C**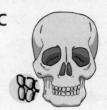

type of tooth	shape of tooth	job of tooth
A incisor	thin, flat with sharp upper edge	cutting food cropping grass
B canine	pointed and sharp	tearing food such as meat
C molar	flat upper surface	grinding and chewing food

Herbivores eat grass, so they have well developed incisors and molars.
Carnivores eat meat, so they have well developed canines.

SATs practice

The pictures at the top of the page show different types of teeth.

LEVEL 3 Animals use teeth for... Tick the **two** correct boxes.

smiling ☐   eating ☐   attacking ☐

growing ☐   sleeping ☐   drinking ☐

LEVEL 4 What type of tooth is used to grind and chew food?

_____

LEVEL 5 The tiger has well developed canine teeth. Explain why.

_____

Caring for your teeth

Bacteria live in your mouth. They feed on sugary foods that stick to your teeth. The bacteria produce **plaque**. It is this plaque that causes tooth decay. To prevent tooth decay and gum disease, you should:

* brush your teeth twice a day
* use floss and mouthwash as well as toothpaste
* visit your dentist every six months
* avoid eating too many sugary foods.

SATs practice

A group of children record when they brush their teeth.

child's name	before breakfast	after breakfast	after school	before bed
Scott	✓		✓	
Rachael		✓		✓
Tim	✓			

LEVEL 3 Which child is most likely to have **tooth decay**?

_____

LEVEL 4 **a** Which child is most likely to have **healthy teeth**?

_____

b Give a reason for your answer.

_____

_____

LEVEL 5 **a** Explain how brushing your teeth helps to prevent tooth decay.

_____

b Write down **one other** way of preventing tooth decay.

_____

The skeleton

Why do you have a skeleton?

You need a skeleton for:

- support   holds your body upright,
- protection   the bones protect important organs,
- movement   bones, with joints and muscles, help you to move.

SATs practice

Humans have a skeleton.

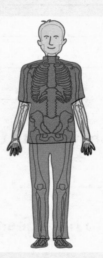

LEVEL 3 Which of the following is a job of your skeleton? Tick the correct box.

controlling your body ☐

taking in food ☐

holding your body upright ☐

LEVEL 4 Which part of the skeleton protects the heart and lungs?

_____

LEVEL 5 Your skeleton helps you to move. Bones cannot move. What else does your skeleton need for movement?

_____

Different bones of the skeleton

We have lots of different bones.
Bones are a different shape according to the job they do.
Bones needed for support are larger, such as leg bones.
Your skull protects your brain, so it needs to be strong and cover all of the brain.

Your ribs protect the lungs and heart, but they need to move each time we breathe, so they are made up of a lot of smaller bones.

SATs practice

The diagram shows a human skeleton.

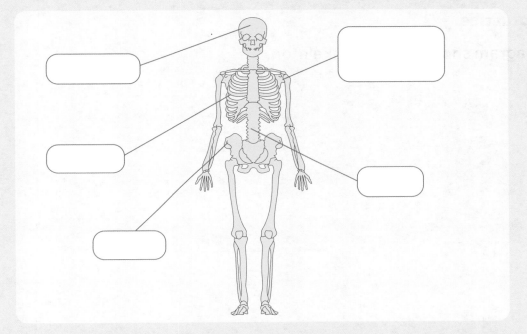

LEVEL 3 Label the skeleton. Choose your words from this list.

| pelvis | ribs | shoulder blade | skull | spine |

LEVEL 4 Which bone protects the brain?

_____

LEVEL 5 The leg bones are long and thick. Explain why.

_____

_____

Joints and muscles

Joints

A bone cannot move.
Joints and muscles cause movement.
A joint is where two or more bones **come together**.
Your elbow and your knee are examples of hinge joints.
These joints move like a door on a door hinge.
Your shoulder and hip are examples of ball-and-socket joints.
These joints allow more movement than hinge joints.

SATs practice

The diagram shows a human skeleton.

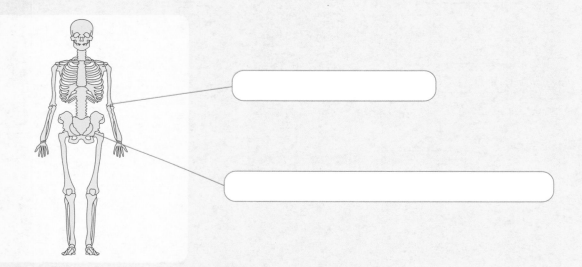

3 On the diagram, write the type of joint in the boxes. Use these words for your labels.

> **ball-and-socket joint**   **hinge joint**

4 Which joint allows most movement?

_____

5 What is a joint?

_____

Muscles

Muscles pull bones to make movement.
Muscles need to work in pairs because they can pull but not push.
To raise your lower arm, your biceps muscle pulls on the bone.
To straighten your arm, your triceps muscle pulls on the bone.
As one muscle becomes shorter, the other muscle relaxes.

SATs practice

Ben is moving his arm.

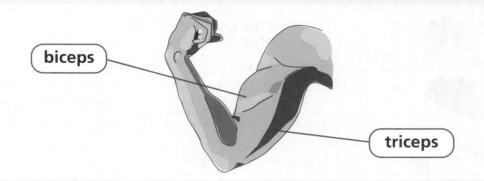

LEVEL 3 How do muscles move bones? Circle the correct word.

> pulling   pushing   pressing

LEVEL 4 Which muscle will be used to straighten the arm?

_____

LEVEL 5 Explain why muscles need to work in pairs.

_____

_____

Healthy diet

What my food is for

We need food, air and water to live.
Different types of food do different jobs in our body.
A healthy diet has a small amount of each of the different types of food.

food	job of the food	food group
 	for growth and repair	protein
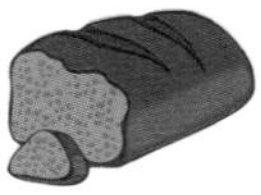	main source of energy	carbohydrates (sugar and starch)
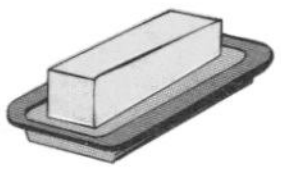 	to provide a store of energy	fats
 	for a healthy body, helps to digest food	fibre, vitamins and minerals

SATs practice

Use the table to help you answer these questions.

LEVEL 3 How is milk and cheese used by the body? Tick the correct box.

for growth and repair ☐

as a main source of energy ☐

to help to digest food ☐

LEVEL 4 Name a food that provides a main source of energy.

_____

LEVEL 5 What is a healthy diet?

_____

_____

Unhealthy diets

It is unhealthy to have too much of any one type of food.
Some foods contain high levels of salt, sugar and fat. You should only have small amounts of these foods.

Some adults have unhealthy diets and lifestyles.
Adults who drink too much alcohol, smoke or take drugs become unhealthy.

SATs practice

 Which one of the following best describes a healthy diet? Tick the correct box.

eating a small amount ☐   not eating sweets ☐
of each type of food

eating mainly fresh ☐   eating lots of chips ☐
fruit and vegetables

 Types of food and how the body uses the food are shown in two lists. Draw straight lines to match the food with its correct use.

meat, fish and cheese		source of energy
fresh fruit and vegetables		growth and repair
cakes, biscuits, bread and pasta		healthy body and to help digestion

 Jenny wants to stay healthy. She does not want an unhealthy diet. Write down **two** things that would make an unhealthy diet.

1 _____

2 _____

Looking at materials

What are materials?

All objects are made up of a **material**.
There are lots of different materials.

object	material
door	wood
window	glass
jumper	wool
saucepan	metal
house	bricks

SATs practice

Jane has some objects to sort into groups.

3 Which one of these materials will burn? _____

4 Jane uses a key to sort the materials. Finish the key by writing the word **glass, paper** or **steel** in the correct box at the bottom of the key.

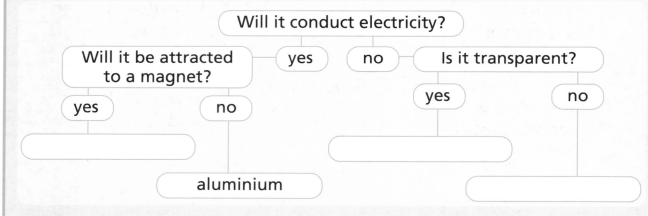

Will it conduct electricity?

Will it be attracted to a magnet? — yes | no — Is it transparent?

yes | no | yes | no

aluminium

5 Write **two** properties of aluminium, using the key to help you.

1 _____

2 _____

Choosing materials

Different materials have different properties.

Properties are things like:
- hard/soft
- conducts electricity/cannot conduct electricity
- conducts heat/cannot conduct heat
- magnetic/non-magnetic
- flexible/brittle

When objects are made, the properties
of the material must match its use.

A mattress made of stone will not be very comfortable.
A door made of paper will not be very strong.

SATs practice

The picture shows some objects made of different materials.

 The coat has a woolly inside because it...
Tick the correct box to finish the sentence.

conducts electricity ☐

keeps heat in ☐

is magnetic ☐

 The lists show the objects and properties of materials. Draw a line to
match each object with a suitable property.

| window | coin | coat |

| warm | transparent | hard |

 Write down **two** properties of metal saucepans.

1 _____

2 _____

Rock and soil types

Uses of rocks and soils

Rocks are everywhere. You can see them lying on the ground, or as cliffs and hills. Rocks are also hidden under the soil.

Soil has tiny particles of rock in it. Sand is made up of tiny particles of rocks or shells.

Some of the uses of rocks include:

• houses • walls • bridges • statues • glass (made from sand)

Rocks are grouped according to their hardness. Chalk is very soft. It is used to make cement. Granite is very hard. It is often used for buildings.

SATs practice

James carried out a scratch test on some rocks. He used three different things to try and scratch the rocks. The table shows his results.

rock	scratched by . . .		
	iron nail	plastic knife	matchstick
granite	x	x	x
chalk	✓	✓	x
marble	✓	x	x

3 Which rock was scratched with a plastic knife? _____

4 James said that granite is the hardest rock. Give a reason for his decision.

_____

5 Write the name of each rock in a box, to show the order of hardness. Start with the hardest rock.

hardest rock —————————————————→ softest rock

Science answer booklet

PLANTS

FLOWERING PLANTS

PAGE 4 The structure of the flowering plant

③
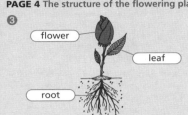
flower
leaf
root

④

part of plant	the job it does
stem	Carries food and water to different parts of the plant.
leaf	Where food is made for the plant.
root	Anchors the plant into the ground.
flower	Where reproduction takes place.

⑤ a Any one of the following: when the plants grow, they will need more space; the roots will spread; the plants will need to compete for water/minerals; the plants will need to compete for sunlight.
   b Any one of the following: food for the plant is made in the leaves; no leaves will mean less food is made; the food is used for growth.

PAGE 5 Inside the flower

③

petal
stigma
stamen

④ Reproduction takes place in the <u>flower</u>. When the flower is in bud, it is protected by the <u>sepal</u>. Pollen lands on the sticky <u>stigma</u>. Pollen is made and stored in the <u>stamen</u>.
⑤ Petals are brightly coloured and scented to attract insects.

WHAT PLANTS NEED TO GROW

PAGE 6 Photosynthesis

③ light and water should be circled
④ photosynthesis should be circled
⑤ Either of the following: so that the plant gets the maximum amount of light; so that more photosynthesis can take place.

PAGE 7 Plants need water

③ water should be circled
④ Any one of the following: same type of plants; same size of plant; same size pots; same type of soil; same amount of soil; left in same position; same amount of light; same temperature; same length of time.
⑤ Plant B will grow best. Plants need some water to live, but too much water will kill the plant.

PAGE 7 Plants need light

③ water and light should be ticked
④

A dry place with very little water.
A dark shady place with very little light and water.
A place with lots of sunlight and water.

⑤ Any of the following: the plants are in the shade of the tree and are not getting enough light; the tree is absorbing all the water/moisture from the soil, so the plants are not getting enough water; the tree is absorbing all the minerals in the soil; the roots from the tree are taking up a lot of space in the soil, so the roots of the plants cannot spread out.

HOW PLANTS REPRODUCE

PAGE 8 Pollination

③ the anther should be circled
④ The other method is wind.
⑤ Any one of the following: colourful petals; scent; nectary at base of carpel; sticky stigma; anther at top of flower; stigma close to top of flower.

PAGE 9 Fertilisation

③ the stigma should be circled
④ The name of the process is fertilisation.
⑤ The pollen grain grows a pollen tube and the male cells move down the pollen tube.

SEED DISPERSAL

PAGE 10 Why do seeds disperse?

③ seed dispersal should be ticked
④ C
⑤ This plant is not in competition with the big tree for water and/or space and/or light.

PAGE 11 Different methods of seed dispersal

③ animal dispersal should be circled
④ 'Birds spread seeds in their droppings' should be ticked
⑤ Plants need to create lots of seeds, as: a) seeds are needed for new plants to grow and b) not all seeds will land on ground where they can grow. Either of these two answers is acceptable.

LIFE CYCLE OF PLANTS

PAGE 12 Germination

③ Any one of the following: same number of seeds; same type of seeds; same type of dish; same amount of cotton wool; same amount of water; same length of time.
④ temperature should be circled
⑤ More seeds germinated in the classroom.

PAGE 13 Life cycle

③ germination should be circled
④ Seeds grow in the ovary.
⑤ Either of the following: pollen grains are blown by the wind; the pollen grains are carried by insects.

ANIMALS AND ECOSYSTEMS

LIFE CYCLE OF HUMANS

PAGE 14 Human life cycle

③ adult
④ baby
⑤ 12 – 18 years should be circled

PAGE 15 Metamorphosis

③ pupa
④ ladybird
⑤ So the animal has plenty to eat at each stage OR less competition for food supply.

PAGE 15 The importance of reproduction

③ zoo should be circled
④ panda should be circled
⑤ The animal or plant is about to die out OR no more will be left.

CLASSIFICATION KEYS

PAGE 16 Using classification keys

③ A = wasp
   B = spider
   C = ant
④ no
⑤ body not divided into 2 parts and has 8 legs

PAGE 17 Venn diagrams

③ A into 3rd section – has 6 legs
   B into 1st section – has wings
   C into centre – both of the above
④ 6 legs and no wings
⑤ 6 legs, wings

PROCESSES OF LIFE

PAGE 18 The seven processes of life

③ breathing should be circled
④ Any one of the following; move, breathe or respire, feel or sense things, grow, reproduce, produce waste or excrete, feed.
⑤ The plant makes its own food through photosynthesis.

PAGE 19 Is it alive?

③ growing should be circled
④ moving
⑤ To be alive, the soldier would need to show all seven life processes.

HARMFUL MICRO-ORGANISMS

PAGE 20 What is a micro-organism?

③ temperature should be circled
④ Any one of the following: same size of bread; same type of bread; all in a plastic bag; left for the same length of time.
⑤ The higher the temperature, the greater the amount of mould.

PAGE 21 Harmful micro-organisms

③ air should be circled
④ Temperature is too low for micro-organisms to grow or reproduce or live.
⑤ Micro-organisms are destroyed at high temperatures, so micro-organisms will not grow.

HELPFUL MICRO-ORGANISMS

PAGE 22 What micro-organisms need to grow

③ observation should be circled
④ air, warmth and water should be ticked
⑤ The mould killed the bacteria.

PAGE 22 Micro-organisms in food production

③ temperature should be circled
④ Any of the following: same amount of flour or yeast or water or time.
⑤ The higher the temperature, the greater the growth of yeast.

PAGE 23 Micro-organisms and decay

③ glass bottles and plastic bags should be ticked
④ Micro-organisms feed on the materials.
⑤ Otherwise there would be too much waste or too many dead plants and animals lying around.

HABITATS

PAGE 24 What is a habitat?
③ Circle around one of the following: butterfly, bird, cabbage, tree.
④ habitat should be circled
⑤ butterfly, bird, cabbage and tree (all needed for one mark)

PAGE 24 Animals in their habitat
③

④ Answer should be any other living thing, such as: pondweed, fish, frog, newt, etc.
⑤ Any one of the following: streamlined body to help tadpole to swim; gills so tadpole can breathe in, the water; tail to move tadpole through the water; (accept: valve to regulate water entering body).

PAGE 25 Plants in their habitat
③
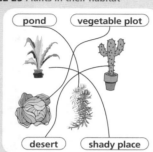
④ Either of the following: so plants can grow bigger or healthier; to provide minerals or nutrients for the plants. (Do not accept: to provide food for the plants.)
⑤ Any one of the following: this plant does not have enough sunlight; the plant leaves are growing long and thin in a search for sunlight; pale leaves because there is too little sunlight.

FOOD CHAINS

PAGE 26 Producers
③ plant should be circled
④ sunlight
⑤ Any two of the following: the eggs are attached to leaves of the plant; the larva feeds on leaves; the pupa attaches itself to leaves; aphids (small insects) live on the plant and ladybirds eat aphids.

PAGE 27 Food chains show feeding relationships
③ corn should be ticked
④ mouse
⑤ Any one of the following: tertiary consumer, carnivore, predator, secondary consumer.

FOOD WEBS

PAGE 28 Lots of food chains
③ dandelion and lettuce should be circled
④ fox
⑤ Animals eat plants, then the animal is eaten by another animal OR energy passes through the food chain as animals eat plants or other animals.

PAGE 29 Changes to food webs
③ rabbit and snail should be ticked
④ Any one of the following: they will move to another place; they will have to eat more dandelions; they will have to find something else to eat. (Accept: they might die. Do not accept: they will have less food.)

⑤ Any one of the following: there will be fewer dandelions; there will be less rabbits, snails, foxes, birds.

ANIMALS ARE ADAPTED TO THEIR ENVIRONMENT

PAGE 30 Penguins
③ penguin, fox
④ Any one of the following: soft, fluffy feathers close to their body; waterproof feathers on the surface; streamlined body.
⑤ Any one of the following: to keep body heat in; to protect penguin from water; to help penguin to swim.

PAGE 31 Camels
③ flat, wide feet and leathery eyelids should be ticked
④ They have a fatty hump on their back which is a store of food and water.
⑤ Any one of the following: long roots, thick stems, narrow leaves (or spines), covered with thick waterproof layer. Explanation to match adaptation: to reach more water; to store water; to reduce water loss.

HUMANS

THE HEART AND THE CIRCULATORY SYSTEM

PAGE 32 The heart
③ heart should be circled
④ the ribcage
⑤ The muscle walls of the heart squeeze together to force blood out of the heart and around the body.

PAGE 33 Blood vessels
③

④ Ticked answers should be:
Blood is carried away from the heart in arteries.
Blood is carried back to the heart in veins.
⑤ Blood is constantly being forced out of the heart along the arteries.

BLOOD

PAGE 34 What does blood do?
③ heart should be circled
④ oxygen should be ticked
⑤ Food and oxygen are needed for cells to make energy (respiration).

PAGE 35 Pulse rates
③ how fast your heart is beating should be ticked
④ Her pulse rate returned to normal (resting pulse rate).
⑤ Any one of the following: Jane's body has used more energy; more energy is needed by Jane's body; more oxygen and food are needed in the muscle cells to make energy; the heart beats faster to provide the extra oxygen and food; increase in respiration.

TEETH

PAGE 36 Types of teeth and their job
③ attacking and eating should be ticked
④ molars
⑤ The tiger eats other animals and needs to tear its food.

PAGE 37 Caring for your teeth
③ Tim
④ a Rachael
   b Any one of the following: If food is removed from teeth after breakfast, then they will be clean all day OR If food is removed from teeth before bed, they will be clean all through the night OR Teeth are kept clean inbetween eating.
⑤ a Brushing removes the sugary food/bacteria/plaque.
   b Any one of the following: visit the dentist; use floss and mouthwash; eat fewer sugary foods.

THE SKELETON

PAGE 38 Why do you have a skeleton?
③ holds your body upright should be ticked
④ ribs
⑤ joints and muscles

PAGE 39 Different bones of the skeleton
③
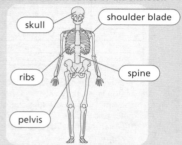
④ skull
⑤ The leg bones need to support all of the body.

JOINTS AND MUSCLES

PAGE 40 Joints
③
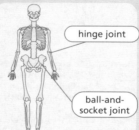
④ ball-and-socket joint
⑤ A joint is where two or more bones come together.

PAGE 41 Muscles
③ pull should be circled
④ triceps
⑤ Muscles work in pairs because they can only pull and not push, so to straighten the body a different muscle must pull the bone back.

HEALTHY DIET

PAGE 42 What my food is for
③ growth and repair should be ticked
④ Any one of the following: bread, pasta, cakes, biscuits, sweets.
⑤ Eating a small amount of each type of food.

PAGE 43 Unhealthy diets
③ Eating a small amount of each type of food should be ticked.
④ meat, fish and cheese – growth and repair
fresh fruit and vegetables – healthy body and to help digestion cakes, biscuits, bread and pasta – source of energy

⑤ Any two of the following:
Too much of any one type of food,
Not enough of any type of food.
Less than 5 a day of fresh fruit and
vegetables.
Too much salt, sugar or fat.
Treating your body badly with smoking,
taking drugs and too much alcohol.

MATERIALS

LOOKING AT MATERIALS

PAGE 44 What are materials?
③ paper towel
④ steel, glass and paper
⑤ Aluminium will conduct electricity but it is not magnetic.

PAGE 45 Choosing materials
③ keeps heat in should be ticked
④ window   transparent
coin   hard
coat   warm
⑤ Any two of the following: conducts heat, hard, rigid.

ROCK AND SOIL TYPES

PAGE 46 Uses of rocks and soils
③ chalk
④ It could not be scratched by any of the equipment (things).
⑤ granite   marble   chalk

PAGE 47 Types of soil
③ soil A should be circled
④ Any one answer from the following:
Same amount of water, same amount of soil, same type of equipment, same time
⑤ Peat = C Sand = A mixture of chalky soil and sand = B

DISSOLVING

PAGE 48 Soluble materials
③ C should be circled
④ A = gravel, B = chalk, C = sugar
⑤ Any one answer from the following:
The solution has become saturated.
There are no more spaces between the water particles.
No more solid could fit into the spaces between the water particles.

PAGE 49 Speeding up dissolving
③ temperature of water should be circled
④ Any one answer from the following:
amount of water, amount of salt, not stirring (or stirring with same force), type of salt.
⑤ yes should be ticked
At 20°C it took 15 minutes for salt to dissolve, but at 80°C it only took 2 minutes for the salt to dissolve.

SEPARATING MATERIALS 1
SIEVING AND FILTERING

PAGE 50 Sieving
③ A sieve is the best choice.
④ The sand and the salt will both pass through the holes in the sieve.
⑤ Add water to the mixture and stir to dissolve the salt, then filter the mixture. The sand will remain on the filter paper.

PAGE 51 Filtering
③ dissolve should be circled
④ The sugar has dissolved in the water, so the sugar solution can pass through the holes in the filter paper.
⑤ They need to heat the sugar solution to evaporate the water vapour.

SEPARATING MATERIALS 2
EVAPORATING AND DISTILLING

PAGE 52 Evaporation
③ dissolving should be circled
④ She can filter the mixture.
⑤ Water evaporated OR water was given off as water vapour.

PAGE 53 Distillation
③ evaporating and condensing should be ticked
④ Because the change is reversible OR they can change back into what they were at the start.
⑤ The water vapour leaves the mixture, leaving the ink in the flask. The water vapour cools as it passes down the tube and the condensation is clean water.

MATERIALS THAT CONDUCT HEAT

PAGE 54 Conducting heat
③ heat should be circled
④ Either of the following:
one spoon is longer than the others; it will take longer for heat to travel through the longer spoon.
⑤ a metal spoon should be ticked
   b Any one answer from:
metal is a good thermal conductor;
metal conducts heat quicker than the other materials;
heat travels through the metal faster than the other materials.

PAGE 55 Uses of thermal conductors
③ It conducts heat should be ticked
④ Heat is conducted through the saucepan and causes the solid chocolate to melt and change into liquid.
⑤ Wood is a poor conductor of heat, so you will not burn yourself on the handle.

THERMAL INSULATORS

PAGE 56 Keeping the heat in
③ thermometer should be ticked
④ Any two answers from: same size beakers; beakers of same material; same amount of water; same starting temperature; same length of time.
⑤ a cotton wool should be ticked
   b There is more air trapped in the cotton wool and air is a good thermal insulator.

PAGE 57 Uses of thermal insulators
③ keep warm should be ticked
④ thermal insulators (accept: insulators)
⑤ More air will be trapped between the layers of clothes and air is a good thermal insulator.

REVERSIBLE CHANGES

PAGE 58 Changing state
③ solid should be circled
④ a kitchen
   b Heat is needed for melting. Most of the ice had melted (or turned into a liquid) in the kitchen.
⑤ The material can be changed back to what it was at the start OR the fruit juice can be frozen again/the frozen juice can melt back to a liquid.

PAGE 59 The water cycle
③ solid should be circled
④ melting
⑤ As water evaporates from the sea, the salt is left behind.

IRREVERSIBLE CHANGES

PAGE 60 Mixing and reacting
③ beaker A
④ Heat the solution to evaporate the water.
⑤ a beaker B
   b Bubbles are shown, so a gas is being given off OR a chemical reaction has taken place and a gas is being given off.

PAGE 61 Heating
③ observation
④ irreversible, irreversible, reversible
⑤ When the butter cools it will be back to its original state.

PHYSICAL PROCESSES

TYPES OF FORCES

PAGE 62 Gravity
③ Newtons should be circled
④ 15
⑤ The greater the mass the greater the weight OR mass and weight are both increasing.

PAGE 63 Friction
③ concrete floor
④ friction
⑤ This is a smoother surface, so there is less friction.

EFFECTS OF FORCES

PAGE 64 Balanced and unbalanced forces
③ gravity should be circled
④ The upthrust of the water is equal to the force of gravity, so the forces are balanced.
⑤ Tim's kicking creates a push force which is greater than the other forces, so he moves forwards.

PAGE 65 Force diagrams
③

④ The force pushing the ball forwards is greater than the other forces, so the ball will move.
⑤ The push force is the same as the force of friction, or the forces are now balanced, so the ball is still.

ELECTRICITY

PAGE 66 Electricity in the home
③ B = glass
C = metal
④ Electricity needs to flow through this part OR electricity flows through this part to provide light.
⑤ Electricity can flow through water, so you could get an electric shock.

PAGE 67 Batteries
③ bulb = B
battery = C
switch = A
④ battery
⑤ The switch is open, so electricity cannot flow around the circuit.

ELECTRICAL CIRCUITS

PAGE 68 Complete circuits
③ B
④ This is a complete circuit.

⑤ Circuit A – Connect wire to other side of battery.
Circuit C – Close the switch.
Circuit D – Join the gap in the wire.

PAGE 69 Brighter and faster
③ length of wire should be ticked
④ Any one of the following: same battery, same bulb, same type of wire, same thickness of wire.
⑤ The shorter the wire, the brighter the bulb OR the longer the wire, the dimmer the bulb.

SOUND

PAGE 70 Vibrations
③ vibrations should be circled
④ The sound becomes quieter.
⑤ Any one of the following: air, wood, brick (accept any other suitable building materials).

PAGE 71 Insulating loud sounds
③ sound level should be ticked
④ polystyrene
⑤ Any one of the following: to act as a comparison; so they would know what the sound level is without insulation; so they can see if insulation made a difference.

PAGE 71 Pitch
③ louder should be circled
④ The sound will become quieter.
⑤ It is a higher pitch.

LIGHT

PAGE 72 Sources of light
③ computer screen should be ticked
④ Light levels become less or lower.
⑤ Any answer from the following: someone may have switched on the light (torch, computer screen, etc); the sun shone through the window; someone opened the door and light entered from the corridor.

PAGE 73 Shadows
③ the distance of the doll from the light source should be ticked
④ The height of the shadow or the size of the shadow.
⑤ The closer the doll to the light source the larger the shadow will be (or similar wording).

RAY DIAGRAMS

PAGE 74 Drawing the path of light
③ Sun should be circled
④ One continuous arrow from Sun to Moon, with arrowhead pointing to Moon.
One continuous arrow from Moon to person on Earth, with arrowhead pointing to person.
⑤ Light from the Sun is reflected off the Moon.

PAGE 75 Reflecting light
③ stage lights should be ticked
④ It reflects or is reflected.
⑤

ATTRACT AND REPEL

PAGE 76 Magnets
③ The N pole and S pole are together should be ticked
④ a They repel.
b Similar poles are together OR similar poles repel.
⑤ The N pole of the magnet always points towards the Earth's north.

PAGE 77 What materials do magnets attract?
③ Steel paper clip and iron key should be ticked
④ Accept any number between 7 and 10.
⑤ The greater the number of magnets, the greater the force of attraction OR the more magnets, the more discs could be picked up (accept similar wording).

EARTH, SUN AND MOON

PAGE 78 Modelling the Earth, Sun and Moon
③ Sun should be circled
④ Move the ball around the lamp in a circular (or oval) shape, in an anticlockwise direction.
⑤ The Earth rotates, so the side facing towards the Sun will have day time and the side facing away from the Sun will have night time.

PAGE 79 Changing shadows
③ opaque should be circled
④ D should be circled
⑤ The Sun appears to move across the sky because the Earth is rotating.

DAY AND NIGHT

PAGE 80 Spinning Earth
③ Sun should be circled
④ C = 12:00 midday
B = 6:00 early evening
A = 12:00 midnight
⑤ The Earth rotates, so the side facing towards the Sun will have day time and the side facing away from the Sun will have night time.

PAGE 81 Changing Moon
③ The Moon reflects light from the Sun should be ticked
④ One continuous arrow from Sun to Moon, with arrowhead pointing to the Moon and one continuous arrow from Moon to person on Earth, with arrowhead pointing to person.
⑤ Because the Moon orbits the Earth so we are seeing the Moon at different positions.

THE SEASONS

PAGE 82 Orbiting Earth
③ Small circle drawn somewhere close to the Earth.
④ Arrows pointing anticlockwise, showing circular or oval orbit around the Sun.
⑤ one year or 365 days

PAGE 83 Our year
③ 4 should be ticked
④ The following answers should be ticked:
The Earth orbits the Sun.
The Earth is tilted on its axis.
⑤ The northern hemisphere is tilting towards the Sun (accept similar wording).

SCIENCE INVESTIGATIONS

PLANNING

PAGE 84 Fair tests
③ stirring should be circled
④ Any two of the following: amount of water, temperature of water, type of container, type of jelly, amount of jelly.
⑤ Any one of the following:
They will time how long it takes for the jelly to dissolve; they will time how long it takes until they can no longer see the solid jelly; they will use a stopwatch and time how long it takes for the jelly to dissolve.

PAGE 85 Making predictions
③ Ticked answers should be:
The temperature of the water
The amount of water
④ EITHER to make it a fair test OR so they know which factor caused the results.
⑤ The smaller the cube of jelly, the faster it will dissolve.
For extra marks: because there will be more jelly in contact with the water.

COLLECTING RESULTS

PAGE 86 Results tables
③ °C should be circled
④ 80°C
⑤ Hope's Results
Any one from:
She has stated the temperature,
She recorded the time in seconds.

PAGE 87 Reliable results
③ stopwatch should be circled
④ Reading for 20 cm, 98 seconds.
⑤ 10 + 14 + 12 = 36   12 seconds

WRITING CONCLUSIONS

PAGE 88 Patterns in results
③ 2
④ The results will be more reliable.
⑤ The smaller the pieces of jelly, the faster they dissolve because more jelly is in contact with the water.

PAGE 89 Scientific reasons
③ force meter should be circled
④ less or smaller amount
greater or more
⑤ As the shoe moves over the rougher surface, there is more friction.

WRITING EVALUATIONS

PAGE 90 Evaluating the method
③ stirring should be circled
④ EITHER to make if a fair test OR because they might stir differently.
⑤ Any two of the following: use a different measuring jug, use a measuring cylinder, have the same person doing the stirring, make sure they cannot see any more jelly in the solution before stopping the stop clock.

PAGE 91 Evaluating the results
③ Time taken for jelly to dissolve should be ticked
④ Set 2 should be circled
40°C
⑤ Any two answers from:
Repeat the reading in set 2 at 40°C.
The results are reliable because they were repeated and an average was calculated.
The average time taken still shows a pattern.

Types of soil

The properties of different soils depend upon the base rock the soil is made from.

type of soil	properties of soil
sandy soil	large particles, water drains through easily, pale colour
clay soil	tiny particles, water does not drain through easily, becomes very sticky when wet, when dry cracks form on the surface
chalky soil	large particles, water drains through easily, pale colour, poor soil, not many plants can grow in it
peat	made from decayed plant material, rather than rock, holds lots of water, dark and crumbly

SATs practice

Class 6A are investigating how water passes through different soils of the same amount. They add 100 cm³ of water to each funnel. They measure how much water passes through after 10 minutes. The picture shows their results.

soil A   soil B   soil C

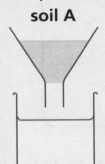 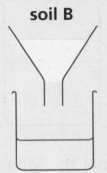 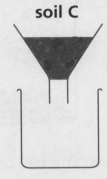

 Which soil allows most water to pass through? Circle the correct answer.

> soil A   soil B   soil C

 Class 6A want to make this a fair test. Write down one thing class 6A do to make this a fair test.

_____

 Write **A**, **B** or **C** in the boxes next to the correct soil.

peat ☐   sand ☐   mixture of chalky soil and sand ☐

Dissolving

Soluble materials

Some materials, such as sugar, **dissolve** in water. When materials dissolve, they combine with the water particles. Materials that dissolve are called **soluble**. Soluble materials form clear solutions.

Some materials, such as sand, cannot dissolve. These materials are called **insoluble**. When insoluble materials are added to water, they can still be seen.

Some materials are more soluble than others. If you keep adding soluble materials to water, eventually no more will dissolve. All of the spaces between the water particles are full, so no more solid can combine with the water. This is called a **saturated** solution. Water with no materials dissolved in it is called **pure** water.

SATs practice

Lily is investigating dissolving. She pours 100cm³ of water into each beaker. Lily then adds 5g of each solid to a beaker. She then stirs the water in each beaker 10 times. The pictures show her results.

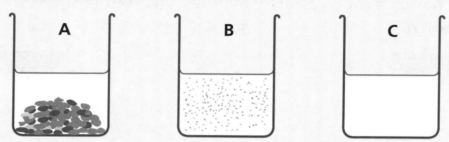

3 One of the beakers shows that the solid has **dissolved**. Circle the letter to show which beaker has a dissolved solid.

A   B   C

4 The solids were sugar, gravel and chalk. Finish the results table. Write in the word **sugar**, **gravel** or **chalk** next to the correct beaker.

beaker	solid added
A	
B	
C	

5 Lily continued to add more of the solid to beaker **C**. Eventually no more solid would dissolve. Explain why.

Speeding up dissolving

Soluble materials can be made to dissolve more quickly by:
- using warmer water
- using more water
- stirring
- cutting material into smaller pieces

SATs practice

Ben is investigating to see if salt dissolves faster in hot water.

LEVEL 3 Ben wants to find out if the temperature of the water affects the time it takes for salt to dissolve. Which **factor** will Ben need to change in his investigation? Circle the correct factor.

> amount of salt   amount of water   temperature of water

LEVEL 4 Ben wants to make this a fair test. Write down **one** thing Ben needs to keep the same to make this a fair test.

_____

LEVEL 5 The table shows Ben's results.

temperature of water (in °C)	time taken to dissolve (in minutes)
20	15
40	11
60	6
80	2

Ben predicted that the hotter the temperature, the faster the salt will dissolve. Does the evidence in the table support Ben's prediction? Tick the correct box, then use the evidence above to support your answer.

yes ☐   no ☐   cannot tell ☐

_____

_____

Separating materials 1 sieving and filtering

Sieving

To separate solids from a liquid, you can use sieving and filtering. A sieve can also be used to separate different size solids, such as soil and stones. Sieves can have different size gaps to suit the job they have to do.

Some of the jobs sieves are used for include:
- separating tea leaves from water
- catching fish
- removing stones and twigs from soil
- removing leaves, twigs and other solids from water
- removing seeds from raspberry jam.

SATs practice

Sammy has a mixture to separate. The mixture contains **pebbles**, **sand** and **salt**. Sammy has some apparatus he can use to separate his mixture.

3 Which piece of apparatus should Sammy use to separate the pebbles from his mixture?

_____

4 Sammy now needs to separate the sand from the salt. Explain why he cannot use the sieve to separate the sand and salt.

_____

5 Describe how Sammy should separate the sand from the salt.

_____

Filtering

Filtering can be used to separate smaller solid particles from a liquid.

A mixture of soluble (will dissolve) and insoluble (will not dissolve) solids can be separated by carrying out the following steps:

- dissolve the soluble solid in water
- filter the mixture
- insoluble solid will be left on filter paper
- solution containing the soluble solid will pass through the filter paper
- evaporate the solution to remove the water
- soluble solid will be left in the evaporating basin.

SATs practice

Class 6B are trying to separate a mixture of **flour** and **sugar**. First of all, they add water to the mixture. Then they stir the mixture well.

 What will happen to the sugar when water is added and the mixture is stirred? Circle the correct word.

condense   dissolve   evaporate

Next, class 6B filter the mixture. The flour stays on the filter paper. Describe what happens to the sugar.

_____

_____

Class 6B are left with a sugar solution. They want just sugar on its own. Describe what they need to do next.

_____

_____

Separating materials 2 evaporating and distilling

Evaporation

A salt solution contains water with salt **dissolved** in it.
To **separate** the salt and water, the solution needs to be heated.
As the solution is heated, **water vapour** (steam) rises from the solution.
The salt (and any other dissolved solid) is left behind.

SATs practice

Kerry is doing an investigation with red sweets. First, she crushes the sweets.

LEVEL 3 Kerry then puts the crushed sweets into a beaker of water and stirs. The water turns red in colour. What is happening to the sweets in the water? Circle the correct word.

> dissolving   evaporating   melting

LEVEL 4 After three hours there are still some larger pieces of sweet in the bottom of the beaker. Describe how Kerry can remove the larger pieces of sweet from the solution.

_____

LEVEL 5 Kerry heats the solution until only red particles are left in the bottom of the dish. Explain what happened to the water.

_____

_____

Distillation

A mixture of two liquids can be separated by **distillation**. As a solution is heated, **water vapour** rises from the solution. This process is called **evaporation**. This water vapour turns back to a liquid when it cools. This process is called **condensation**. These two processes take place in distillation.

SATs practice

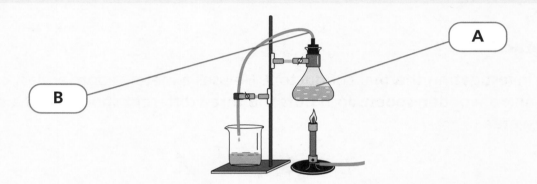

Evaporation is taking place at **A**.
Condensation is taking place at **B**.

James is separating ink from water by distillation.

LEVEL 3 Which two changes of state take place during distillation?
Tick the **two** correct boxes.

melting	☐	condensing	☐
evaporating	☐	freezing	☐
dissolving	☐	filtering	☐

LEVEL 4 Changes of state are **physical** changes. Explain why changing state is a physical change.

_____

LEVEL 5 During distillation, clean water is produced from the ink solution. Explain how the distillation process produces clean water.

_____

_____

Materials that conduct heat

Conducting heat

A metal spoon left in a cup of hot tea will soon feel hot. The metal spoon lets heat travel along it, so it feels hot at the end. Metal is a good **conductor** of heat. Materials that conduct heat well are called **thermal conductors**.

SATs practice

Josh is investigating thermal conductors. He uses a metal spoon, a plastic spoon and a wooden spoon. Josh puts the three different spoons into a mug of hot water.

LEVEL 3 Finish the sentence. Josh is investigating how different materials conduct … Circle the correct word.

> electricity   heat   light

LEVEL 4 Josh thinks his investigation is a fair test. Give **one** reason why this is **not** a fair test.

_____

_____

LEVEL 5 Predict which spoon will be the first to get hot.

a Tick a box.

plastic spoon ☐   metal spoon ☐   wooden spoon ☐

b Give a reason for your answer.

_____

Uses of thermal conductors

Metal is a good thermal conductor.
Saucepans and baking trays are made of metal.
They conduct the heat to your food, so it can cook quickly.

Saucepan handles are made from a different material that will not conduct heat. This stops you burning yourself.

SATs practice

Becky is decorating a cake with chocolate. She uses a metal saucepan to warm the chocolate.

3 Becky puts the chocolate into the saucepan. She puts the saucepan on the cooker to warm the chocolate.

Why is metal a good material for a saucepan? Tick the correct box.

It conducts electricity. ☐

It conducts heat. ☐

It is very heavy. ☐

It is a pretty colour. ☐

4 The chocolate in the saucepan becomes runny. Explain why the chocolate has changed state.

_____

_____

5 The saucepan handle is made of wood. Explain why wood is a good material for a saucepan handle.

_____

Thermal insulators

Keeping the heat in

Thermal insulators keep heat in. Air is a good thermal insulator. Materials that have air trapped in them are good thermal insulators. A coat with a woolly inside, a duvet and a woolly scarf are all good thermal insulators.

SATs practice

Class 5A are investigating how to keep coffee hot. They are using different materials wrapped around the outside of the beakers to see which is best at keeping the coffee hot.

They have three beakers of the same material, a thermometer, a stopwatch, some cotton wool, some paper and some aluminium foil. They set up their apparatus and fill each beaker with hot water. They record the temperature every five minutes.

Cotton wool   Paper   Plastic

LEVEL 3 What equipment do they use to measure the temperature of the water? Tick the correct box.

stopwatch ☐   thermometer ☐   beaker ☐   ruler ☐

LEVEL 4 Class 5A wanted to make this a fair test. Write down **two** things they did to make this a fair test.

1 _____

2 _____

LEVEL 5 Predict which material is the best thermal insulator.

a Tick the correct box.

cotton wool ☐   paper ☐   plastic ☐

b Give a reason for your prediction.

_____

Uses of thermal insulators

Your winter coat keeps you warm. It is a good thermal insulator. Woolly socks, a fleece, woollen mittens and sleeping bags are all good thermal insulators. They all keep heat in.

Food from a take-away is served in polystyrene containers to help it stay warm.

A flask has a shiny inside and air trapped in its outer case. The shiny inside reflects heat back in. The trapped air stops heat from escaping.

Carpets and cork flooring both have air trapped in them, so they are warm.

SATs practice

Sally and George are going out for a walk on a cold day. George is wearing a thick sweater. Sally is wearing several layers of thinner jumpers.

3 Sally and George are trying to …
Tick the correct box.

keep cool	☐
stay clean	☐
keep warm	☐
stay dry	☐

4 Finish the sentence.

Sweaters, jumpers and coats are all good _____

_____.

5 Wearing several layers of clothing will keep you warmer than just one thick sweater. Explain why.

_____

_____

Reversible changes

Changing state

We can make changes to materials. With some changes, we can put them back to what they were at the start. These changes are called reversible changes.

Water can be changed into ice. The ice can then melt back into water. This is a reversible change.

The ice is a solid and the water is a liquid. Solid, liquid and gas are the three states of matter. Materials can exist in each of the states.

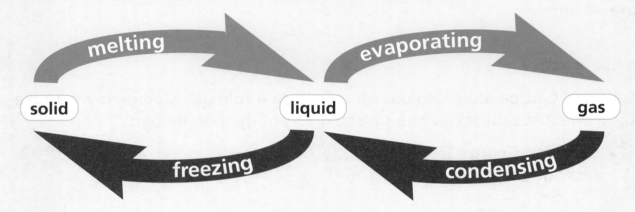

SATs practice

Jenna makes ice lollies. She pours fruit juice into plastic moulds and puts them into the freezer. The next day Jenna takes the ice lollies out of the freezer.

 What is the state of the ice lollies when they are removed from the freezer? Circle the correct answer.

solid   liquid   gas

 Jenna places the lollies into cups. She leaves each cup in a different room. After half an hour Jenna measures the volume of liquid in each cup. The table shows her results.

room	kitchen	bathroom	living room	bedroom
volume of liquid in cm³	15	6	12	10

a Which room was warmest?

____

b Give a reason for your answer.

____

____

LEVEL 5 Explain why this is an example of a reversible change.

____

____

The water cycle

The water cycle shows how water changes state.

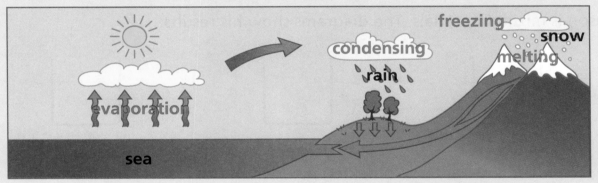

SATs practice

Water changes state as it moves through the water cycle.

LEVEL 3 Water can form as snow. What state is snow? Circle the correct state.

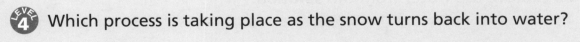

solid **liquid** **gas**

LEVEL 4 Which process is taking place as the snow turns back into water?

____

LEVEL 5 Explain why rain is not salty.

____

____

Irreversible changes

Mixing and reacting

We can cause materials to change. Sometimes these changes cannot be put back to how they were at the start. This type of change cannot be reversed, so it is called **irreversible**. A reaction has taken place to cause this change. Sometimes you can see bubbles as a gas is given off.

Some irreversible changes include mixing:
- plaster of Paris with water
- baking powder with vinegar
- cement with water
- lemon juice with washing soda.

SATs practice

Jason is mixing materials. The diagrams show his results.

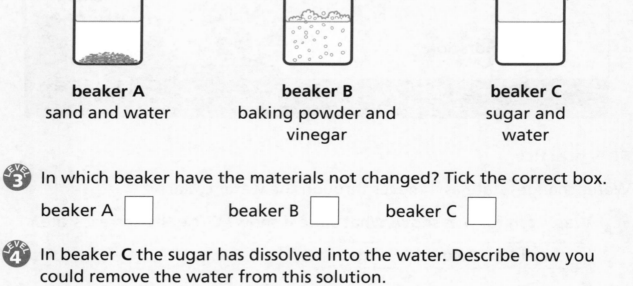

beaker A
sand and water

beaker B
baking powder and
vinegar

beaker C
sugar and
water

LEVEL 3 In which beaker have the materials not changed? Tick the correct box.

beaker A ☐   beaker B ☐   beaker C ☐

LEVEL 4 In beaker **C** the sugar has dissolved into the water. Describe how you could remove the water from this solution.

_____

LEVEL 5 a Which beaker shows an irreversible change? _____

b Give a reason for your answer.

_____

_____

Heating

Some materials change when they are heated up and the material cannot be returned back to its original state. This is an **irreversible change**.

These types of irreversible changes include:
- burning paper
- baking a cake
- frying an egg
- burning a bonfire
- a firework

SATs practice

Class 6A are heating some foods.

The table shows their results.

food	description of food when heated	reversible or irreversible?
butter	melts	reversible
crisp	burns	
egg	changes colour	
chocolate	melts	

3 What word do we use to describe the results Class 6A noted? Tick the correct box.

conclusion ☐   evaluation ☐

observation ☐   measurement ☐

4 Finish the table by writing **reversible** or **irreversible** in the end column. The first one has been done for you.

5 Explain why butter melting is a reversible change.

_____

Types of forces

Gravity

A **force** causes a moving object to change its speed or direction.

Examples of forces are:
- push, pull, turn, twist
- gravity
- friction
- magnetism
- air resistance
- upthrust

Gravity is the force that pulls objects towards the Earth. We have weight because of gravity. The Earth is large with a large mass, so smaller objects are pulled towards it. Our Earth is held in orbit around the Sun. This is because the Earth is smaller than the Sun, so the Earth is pulled towards it.

There is some gravity on the Moon. However, the Moon is smaller than the Earth, so there is less gravity on the Moon than on the Earth.

SATs practice

Michelle uses a force meter to weigh different masses.
The table shows her results.

mass in g	weight in N
200	2
400	4
600	6
800	8
1000	10

 3 What unit is weight measured in? Circle the correct word.

grams   Newtons   kilograms

4 Predict the weight of a 1500g mass. _____ N

5 Explain the relationship between mass and weight.

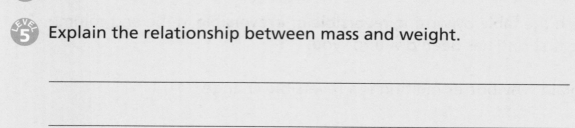

_____

_____

Friction

Friction is the force caused when things are pulled against each other. Smooth surfaces have less friction. Rough surfaces have greater friction.

Friction is useful, as it helps you to walk and stops cars sliding around. When ice is on the ground, there is less friction, so we slide and slip.

SATs practice

Sam is measuring the force needed to pull a shoe across different surfaces.

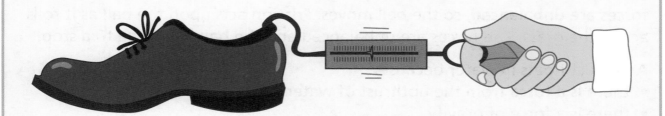

Here are her results.

surface	force in N
carpet	25
smooth table	10
concrete floor	35
plastic sheet covered in oil	3

 Which surface needed the most force to pull the shoe?

_____

 What type of force made it hard to pull the shoe?

_____

 It took less force to move the shoe over the plastic sheet covered in oil than any other surface. Explain why.

_____

_____

Effects of forces

Balanced and unbalanced forces

Several forces are acting upon objects all the time. When an object is still, the forces are **balanced** or equal. When balanced forces act upon a moving object, the object continues to move in the same direction at the same speed.

At the start of a football match, the ball is still because the forces are balanced. When you kick the ball, you give an extra push of force. Now the forces are **unbalanced**, so the ball moves. Friction acts upon the ball as it rolls across the grass. The forces are unbalanced and the ball will come to a stop.

An object floats in water because:
- there is a force from the upthrust of water
- there is a force of gravity
- both of these forces are balanced.

SATs practice

Tim visits the swimming pool. He is floating on the surface of the water.

 Which force is pulling Tim down in the water?
Circle the correct answer.

friction   gravity   upthrust

 Tim is floating in the water, even though a force is pulling him down. Explain why.

_____

_____

 Tim starts to kick his feet and he moves forwards. Explain why Tim is moving forwards.

_____

_____

Force diagrams

It helps to draw arrows onto pictures to show the forces. The direction of the arrow shows the direction of the force. The size of the arrow represents the size of the force.

This diagram shows the ball is still because all four forces acting upon it are equal or balanced.

SATs practice

The diagram shows the forces acting on a ball.

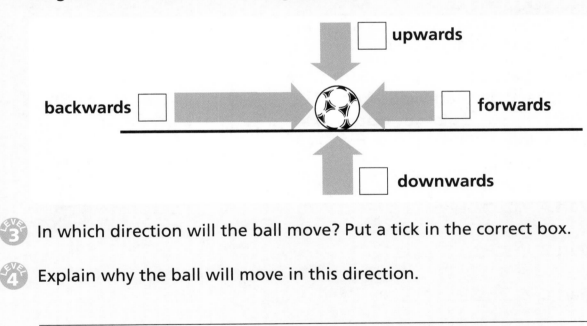

upwards

backwards

forwards

downwards

3 In which direction will the ball move? Put a tick in the correct box.

4 Explain why the ball will move in this direction.

_____

_____

5 The ball rolled along the ground, then stopped. Explain why the ball stopped.

_____

_____

Electricity

Electricity in the home

You use electricity in your home for cooking, light and heat. Electricity from the mains sockets is very dangerous and could kill you.

Never:
- play with electric plugs and sockets
- push things into an electric socket
- touch switches or plugs with wet hands.

The outside of the plug is made from plastic. Plastic is an insulator. Insulators do not allow electricity to flow through them. The metal pins are conductors. Conductors allow electricity to flow through them. Metal is a good conductor of electricity.

SATs practice

The picture shows a light bulb.

3 Parts of the light bulb are made from metal and parts are made from glass. Write the word **glass** or **metal** next to the letters. The first one has been done for you.

Part **A** ____*metal*____

Part **B** _____

Part **C** _____

4 Explain why part **A** must be made with metal.

_____

5 You should never change a light bulb with wet hands. Explain why.

_____

Batteries

Many of your toys and games use electricity from **batteries**.
Inside the battery there are **chemicals** that generate electricity.
Different types of batteries can provide different amounts of electricity.
More powerful batteries give off a greater **voltage**.
When all of the chemicals have reacted, no more electricity can be generated.

When we draw circuit diagrams, we do not draw pictures of the different parts; we use symbols.

This is the circuit symbol for a battery.

Here are some more circuit symbols:

bulb   buzzer   switch

SATs practice

Anna sets up a circuit.
This is a diagram of Anna's circuit.

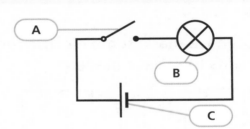

 Name the parts of the circuit.
Write a letter next to each word.
Choose your letters from **A**, **B** or **C**.

circuit part	letter A, B or C
bulb	
battery	
switch	

 Which part of this circuit is providing electricity to light the bulb?

_____

 The bulb in this circuit will not light. Explain why.

_____

_____

Electrical circuits

Complete circuits

Electricity flows through wires. The battery forces the electricity through the wires. The circuit has to be complete for the electricity to flow. Bulbs will light if there is not a break in the circuit. A switch is used to provide a break in the circuit. Electricity cannot flow through an open switch, so the bulb cannot light.

We do not draw the parts of the circuit; we draw the symbols.

 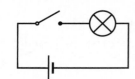

SATs practice

Class 6G have made some electric circuits. Here are the circuit diagrams of the circuits they have made.

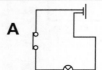   A   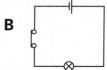   B   C   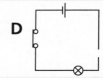   D

3 Only one circuit has a bulb that lights. This circuit is _____. Choose your answer from **A**, **B**, **C** or **D**.

4 Explain why the bulb will light in this circuit.

_____

5 Explain what the children will need to do to the other circuits to get the bulb to light.

Circuit ___ _____

Circuit ___ _____

Circuit ___ _____

Brighter and faster

It is possible to make the bulbs in a circuit shine brighter by adding more batteries.

It is possible to use more powerful batteries.
These bulbs are set up in series.
The bulbs will be brighter if they are set up in parallel.

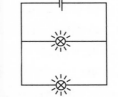

These changes can also make buzzers buzz louder or a motor turn faster.

Adam is investigating electric circuits. He wants to know if the length of wire will affect the brightness of the bulb.

This is the circuit diagram for Adam's investigation.

SATs practice

3 What factor will Adam need to change in his investigation?
Tick the correct box.

thickness of wire ☐   length of wire ☐   colour of wire ☐

4 Write down **one** factor Adam will need to keep the same to make this a fair test.

_____

5 Here are his results.

length of wire in cm	brightness of bulb
50	bright
100	dim glow
150	faint light

Describe the relationship between the length of wire and the brightness of the bulb.

_____

Sound

Vibrations

All sounds are caused by **vibrations**. Sounds can travel through solids, liquids and gases. When you listen to a live band, you hear the drum because:

- the drum skin vibrates when it is hit
- this causes the air around it to vibrate
- the vibrations in the air travel towards your ear
- the air vibrations enter your ear
- these vibrations pass through your ear and send a message to your brain
- your brain recognises the drum sound.

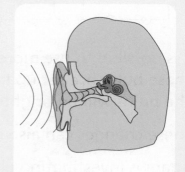

SATs practice

Kerry listens to Joe playing the drum.

 As Joe hits the drum with his drumstick, a sound is made. What causes the sound? Circle the correct word.

> air   sound   vibrations

 Kerry walks into the next room. Describe what happens to the loudness of the drum sound as she walks away.

_____

 Kerry shuts the door. She can still hear the drum. Write down **one** material the sound passes through to travel to Kerry.

_____

Insulating loud sounds

To make a sound louder, the vibrations need to be larger. When you hit a drum harder, the sound is louder. The loudness of sound is measured in decibels (dB). Loud sounds can damage your ears. People working in noisy places protect their ears with ear mufflers. The air trapped inside the mufflers insulates the ear from the sound.

SATs practice

Mrs. Porter's class use a data logger to measure sound levels. They place a radio under different materials.

 What do the class measure? Tick the correct box.

music level ☐   sound level ☐   number of vibrations ☐

 The table shows their results.

material	sound level in decibels
no material	24
polystyrene	11
cotton wool	16

Which material would be most suitable to use inside ear mufflers?

_____

 The class recorded the sound level without any material. Explain why.

_____

Pitch

The pitch of a sound is how high or how low it is. Little girls scream in a **high pitch**. A large drum makes a **low pitch**. The more material vibrating, the lower the pitch. Longer guitar strings have a lower pitch than a shorter guitar string.

SATs practice

Sam is playing the guitar for his friends. When he plucks the string hard, the sound becomes... Circle the correct word.

> quieter   louder   softer

Describe how the sound changes as his friends walk away.

_____

Describe the difference in the note when Sam tightens the string.

_____

Light

Sources of light

Light travels from a source. Examples of light sources are:

- the Sun
- computer screen
- TV screen
- electric lamp
- torch
- candle

Anything that gives out light is a **light source**.

A mirror is not a light source; it **reflects** light. Examples of objects that reflect light are:

- the Moon
- tin foil
- glass
- glitter

If you are not sure whether an object is a light source, try to imagine that object in a dark room. If the object would give out light, then it is a light source.

SATs practice

 Jane uses a light sensor to record light levels in the classroom. Which is a possible source of light in the classroom? Tick the correct box.

desk ☐ computer screen ☐ mirror ☐

Jane places the light sensor in the middle of the classroom.
This chart shows how the light level changes over 10 minutes.

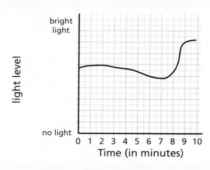

Describe what happens to the light levels between 2 and 7 minutes.

_____

Suggest what might have happened in the classroom at 8 minutes to cause the change on the chart.

_____

Shadows

When an object blocks light, a shadow forms. Materials that form shadows are called opaque. The shadow forms the outline of the object, but no detail or colour. Reflections are different from shadows. Reflections show detail and colour. As the object moves closer to the light source, the shadow becomes taller.

SATs practice

Aimee is investigating how the distance of an object from the light source affects the size of the shadow. Aimee makes a shadow of a doll on the screen.

3 What factor will Aimee change during this investigation?
Tick the correct box.

the size of the doll ☐

the distance of the doll ☐
from the light source

the size of the screen ☐

the distance of the screen ☐
from the light source

4 What factor will Aimee measure to collect her results?

_____

5 Write a prediction for this investigation.

_____

_____

Ray diagrams

Drawing the path of light

Light travels in straight lines. This is why we cannot see around corners.

Light travels from a light source into our eyes. Light does not travel **from** our eyes; it always travels **into** our eyes.

We see objects because:
- the light travels from the source towards the object
- the light then reflects off the object
- the light rays then travel towards our eyes.

When you draw a ray diagram, you must remember:
- use a ruler to draw a straight line
- the rays must be continuous (no breaks in them)
- draw arrowheads on your lines to show the direction the light is travelling in
- light always travels into the eyes.

SATs practice

We see the Moon because light from the Sun reflects off the Moon.

3 In this diagram, which is the source of light? Circle the correct answer.

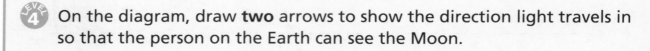

Earth   Moon   Sun

4 On the diagram, draw **two** arrows to show the direction light travels in so that the person on the Earth can see the Moon.

5 Explain why the person on the Earth can see the Moon.

_____

_____

Reflecting light

Light reflects from shiny surfaces. Materials with smooth, shiny surfaces are good reflectors of light. The diagram shows how you see your reflection in a mirror.

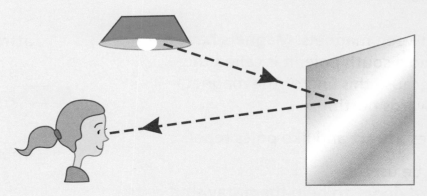

SATs practice

The school children are watching a play.

3 The children can see the actors because of light from a light source. Tick the box to show the light source.

actors ☐   stage lights ☐

stage ☐   speakers ☐

3 James is at the back of the crowd of children. He uses a periscope to see the actors.

4 James can see the actors as the light travels through the periscope. Write down the correct word used to describe what happens to light as it hits the mirrors.

_____

5 On the diagram, draw the path of light through the periscope to show how James can see the actors.

Attract and repel

Magnets

Forces act between magnets. Magnets have a north pole and a south pole. It is called the north pole because this end of the magnet will point towards north.

Opposite poles **attract** and like poles **repel**.

Magnets can be useful:
- on cupboard doors, to help them stay shut
- to help separate different metals (iron is magnetic)
- because they help loudspeakers to work.

attraction

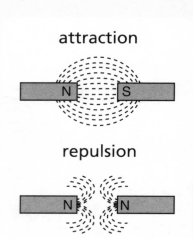

repulsion

SATs practice

Sarah is investigating magnets.

3 Sarah places another magnet close to the magnet in the holder. Why are the two magnets attracted together? Tick the correct box.

The N pole and N pole are together. ☐

The N pole and S pole are together. ☐

The magnet is metal. ☐

4 Sarah turns her magnet around.

a What happens to the two magnets now? _____

b Give a reason for your answer.

_____

_____

5 Sarah notices that the magnet in the holder always points in the same direction. Explain why.

_____

_____

What materials do magnets attract?

Not all metals are magnetic. Only some metals are magnetic. Iron is magnetic. Some alloys (mixtures of metals), with iron in them, are magnetic. Steel is an alloy with iron in it, so steel is magnetic.

Materials that are not attracted to a magnet are called non-magnetic.

magnetic	non-magnetic
key	wood
metal can	candle
iron nail	kitchen foil
iron filings	copper pipe

SATs practice

3 Sayed tests different materials to see which are attracted towards the magnet. Put a tick in the box next to the **two** materials that are magnetic.

wooden ruler ☐   paper worksheet ☐

steel paper clip ☐   cotton skirt ☐

plastic pencil case ☐   iron key ☐

Sayed picks up some metal discs with his magnet. When he holds two magnets together, he can pick up more discs. Sayed repeats his experiment with three magnets. The table shows his results.

number of magnets	number of discs picked up
1	2
2	4
3	6

4 Predict how many discs Sayed could pick up using four magnets.

_____

5 Write a conclusion for Sayed's experiment.

_____

_____

Earth, Sun and Moon

Modelling the Earth, Sun and Moon

The Earth, Sun and Moon are spherical. The Sun is the largest planet and our Moon is the smallest. The Moon orbits the Earth. The Earth and the Moon orbit the Sun.

The Sun, Earth and Moon are too big for us to look at properly. We can use models to represent the Sun, Earth and Moon. We could use a football to model the Sun, a tennis ball to model the Earth and a pea for the Moon.

model of Sun   **model of Earth**   **model of Moon**

SATs practice

Mrs. Clegg is using models to tell class 5 about the Earth, Sun and Moon.

 3 In this model, which part does the lamp represent? Circle the correct answer.

> **Earth**   **Moon**   **Sun**

4 Mrs. Clegg wants to show class 5 the Earth's orbit. Describe what she should do to demonstrate the Earth's orbit.

_____

_____

5 Mrs. Clegg has drawn a cross on the ball, to show Class 5 that they are in daytime. Explain why we have daytime and night-time.

_____

_____

Changing shadows

A stick placed in the ground will form a shadow as the Sun shines on it.
The length of the shadow changes during the day.
Our Earth rotates. This gives the impression that the Sun is moving across the sky.
The shadow of the stick will be longer in the mornings and evenings, when the Sun is low in the sky.
The shadow of the stick is shortest at midday, when the Sun is overhead.

SATs practice

The picture shows the position of the Sun in the sky at different times of the day, labelled **A**, **B**, **C**, **D** and **E**.

The picture also shows a post with its shadow.

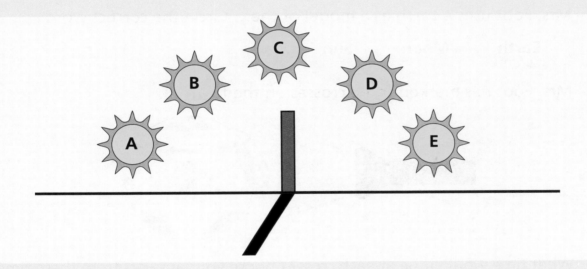

LEVEL 3 The post casts a shadow because it is… Circle the correct answer.

> **opaque**   **solid**   **wood**

LEVEL 4 Which position of the Sun is casting the shadow?
Circle the correct letter.

> **A**   **B**   **C**   **D**   **E**

LEVEL 5 Explain why the Sun seems to move across the sky.

_____

_____

Day and night

Spinning Earth

We have day and night because the Earth rotates.
If our side of the Earth is facing towards the Sun, we are having daytime.
If our side of the Earth is facing away from the Sun, we are in night-time.

It takes 24 hours for the Earth to complete one rotation.

SATs practice

Mrs. Foot tells Class 5 about why we have day and night.
Mrs. Foot uses a torch and a football as models.

LEVEL 3 Mrs. Foot uses a torch as a model of the... Circle the correct word.

> **Earth**   **Moon**   **Sun**

LEVEL 4 Mrs. Foot has marked three crosses on the football.

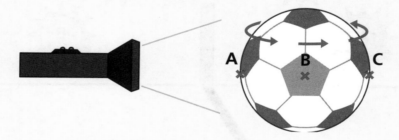

What time would it be at each cross? Choose your answers from these times.

12:00 midnight   **6:00 early morning**

12:00 midday   **6:00 early evening**

At cross **A** it will be _____.

At cross **B** it will be _____.

At cross **C** it will be _____.

LEVEL 5 Explain why we have day and night.

_____

_____

Changing Moon

The Moon orbits the Earth. For the Moon to orbit the Earth once, it takes 28 days. We see the Moon because it reflects light from the Sun. As the Moon orbits the Earth, the amount of light reflected changes. So as the Moon orbits the Earth, it appears to change shape.

SATs practice

Harriet has drawn a picture of the Sun, the Moon and a person standing on the Earth.

3 Harriet says we can see the Moon, even though it does not give out its own light. Why can we see the Moon? Tick the correct box.

The Moon reflects light from the Sun. ☐

The Moon reflects light from the Earth. ☐

The Moon reflects light from space. ☐

4 On the picture, draw **two arrows** to show how the person on the Earth can see the Moon.

5 The Moon appears to change shape during the month. Explain why.

_____

_____

The seasons

Orbiting Earth

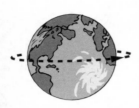

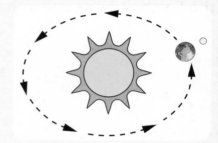

It takes 24 hours for one rotation of the Earth.

It takes 28 days for the Moon to orbit the Earth.

It takes one year (365 days) for the Earth and Moon to orbit the Sun.

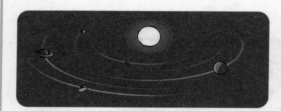

The Sun is the centre of our **Solar System**. All the other planets in our Solar System orbit the Sun.

SATs practice

The diagram shows how the Earth orbits the Sun.

3 On the diagram, draw a small circle to show the position of the Moon.

4 On the diagram, draw arrows to show the Earth's orbit.

5 How long does it take for the Earth to orbit the Sun?

_____

Our year

The Earth is tilted on its axis. This tilt causes the northern hemisphere (top half of the Earth) to point towards the Sun or away from the Sun.

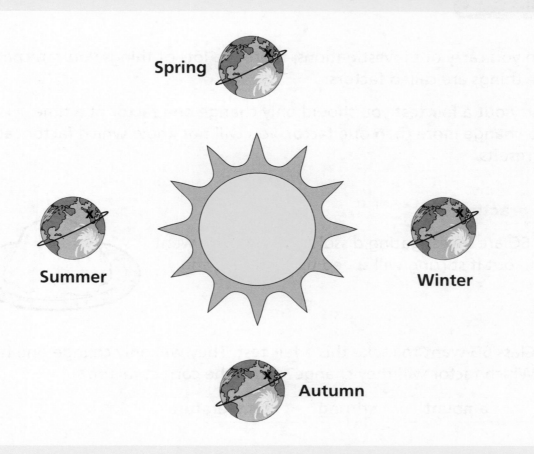

Spring

Summer

Winter

Autumn

SATs practice

 How many seasons do we have in one year? Circle the correct answer.

2 4 6 8

We have different seasons because… Tick **two** boxes.

The Earth rotates. ☐ The Moon orbits the Earth. ☐

The Earth orbits the Sun. ☐ The Sun orbits the Earth. ☐

The Earth is tilted on its axis. ☐ It takes one year to orbit the Sun. ☐

Explain why Spring and Summer are our warmest seasons.

_____

_____

Planning

Fair tests

When you carry out investigations, there are lots of things you can change. These things are called **factors**.

To carry out a **fair test** you should only change **one factor** at a time. If you change more than one factor, you will not know which factor caused your results.

SATs practice

Class 6G are investigating dissolving jelly. They want to find out if stirring will speed up the dissolving.

3 Class 6G want to make this a fair test. They will only change one factor. Which factor will they change? Circle the correct factor.

> amount   stirring   temperature

4 Write down two factors they should keep the same.

1 _____

2 _____

5 How will Class 6G measure their results?

_____

_____

_____

Making predictions

When you write a prediction, you are saying what you expect to happen in your investigation. Always try to give a reason for your prediction.

Example

I think sugar will dissolve quicker in hot water because there are more spaces between the water particles for the sugar to move into.

Try to use this writing frame:

I think . . . . will happen because . . . .

SATs practice

Class 6G are investigating dissolving jelly. They want to find out if the size of the jelly cube will affect the time taken for the jelly to dissolve.

LEVEL 3 Class 6G will change the size of the jelly cubes. Which **two** factors will they keep the same? Tick **two** boxes.

the temperature of the water ☐

the kettle used to boil water ☐

the size of the jelly cube ☐

the time of day ☐

the scissors used to cut the jelly ☐

the amount of water ☐

LEVEL 4 Explain why Class 6G must only change one factor.

_____

_____

LEVEL 5 Write a prediction for this investigation.

_____

_____

Collecting results

Results tables

It is important to draw your results table before you start your experiment. You need to think about what you are going to measure.

Each column must have a heading. Try to include units with your heading, such as:

- time in seconds
- length in cm
- temperature in °C

SATs practice

Matthew and Hope are dissolving jelly in different temperatures of water.

 What is the unit for temperature? Circle the correct answer.

> cm   m   °C   cm³   °T

 Matthew and Hope recorded their results.

Matthew's results

temperature of water	time taken for jelly to dissolve in minutes
cold	8
room temperature	4
hot	1.5

Hope's results

temperature of water in °C	time taken for jelly to dissolve in seconds
20	360
40	140
80	60

At which temperature did the jelly dissolve the fastest? _____

 Whose set of results is most accurate? Tick the correct box.

Matthew's results ☐   Hope's results ☐

Give a reason for your answer.

_____

Reliable results

Occasionally mistakes are made when recording results.
If several sets of readings have been taken, the mistake is more obvious.

When several sets of readings have been taken, it is then possible to calculate the average reading.

To find the average, you:
• add all of your readings together
• divide your answer by the number of times you took a reading.

For example, John recorded three temperatures.

20°C   18°C   21°C

20 + 18 + 21 = 59

59 ÷ 3 = 19   So the average temperature is 19°C.

SATs practice

Ben is timing how long it takes for a car to move down a ramp. Ben increases one end of the ramp.

 What will Ben use to measure the time taken for the car to move down the ramp? Circle the correct piece of equipment.

| ruler   stopwatch   tape measure   thermometer |

Here is Ben's results table.

height of ramp at one end in cm	time taken for car to move down ramp in seconds			average time in seconds
10	48	52	50	50
20	24	98	26	49
30	10	14	12	?
40	3	4	3	3

 Which result seems to be incorrect and why?

_____

 Calculate the average time of the car on the ramp at 30 cm.

_____

Writing conclusions

Patterns in results

When you write a conclusion, you write about what you found out from the experiment. The conclusion often answers the title of the experiment.

Before you start to write your conclusion, you need to look carefully at the results. Try to think of a relationship between the two sets of readings.

SATs practice

Class 6G are investigating how fast they can make jelly dissolve. Each group has one large block of jelly. They cut the block into different size pieces.

Here are the results.

number of pieces cut from one block of jelly	time taken for jelly to dissolve in minutes			average time for jelly to dissolve in minutes
1	20	18	25	21
4	12	10	14	12
8	5	4	6.5	5
16	2	1.5	2.5	2

LEVEL 3 What is the **average time** taken for the jelly to dissolve when it is cut into sixteen small pieces?

_____ minutes

LEVEL 4 Class 6G took three sets of readings and found the average time taken to dissolve the jelly. Explain why.

_____

LEVEL 5 Write a conclusion for this set of results.

_____

_____

Scientific reasons

When you have written your conclusion, it is then important to try and give a reason for your results.

Try to think of a scientific reason for your results.

SATs practice

Ashley is investigating forces. He is measuring the force needed to pull his shoe across different surfaces.

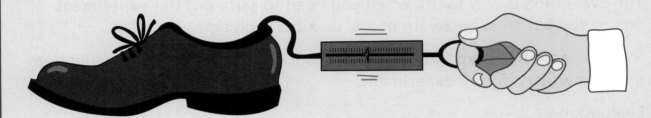

 LEVEL 3 What equipment does Ashley use to measure the force? Circle the correct answer.

> **force meter**   stopwatch   tape measure

Here are Ashley's results.

surface	force in newtons
carpet	7
smooth tiles	2
rough tiles	8
playground	10

LEVEL 4 Finish writing the conclusion for this set of results. Write words into the spaces.

The smoother the surface, the _____ the force needed to pull the shoe.

The rougher the surface, the _____ the force needed to pull the shoe.

 LEVEL 5 Give a scientific reason for this conclusion.

_____

Writing evaluations

Evaluating the method

The evaluation is the final part of your investigation.
You need to think about the method and your results.

In the evaluation, you should write about any problems you had with the method and what went well.

The evaluation is very useful when you need to carry out this experiment again. You will then be aware of any possible problems.

Josh carried out his experiment about dissolving jelly. Here is the evaluation Josh has written for his experiment.

Evaluation

We could not see the numbers on our measuring jugs, so we were not sure how much water we used to dissolve the jelly. It was difficult to tell when all of the jelly had dissolved. I stirred one jug and Jasmine stirred the other. Mrs. Porter said the same person should have done the stirring.

SATs practice

 3 What part of their experiment did Mrs. Porter comment on?
Circle the correct answer.

> jelly   stirring   temperature

4 Why did Mrs. Porter say that only one person should have carried out this part of the experiment?

_____

_____

5 Josh is going to repeat this experiment. Write down **two** things Josh could do to improve his experiment.

1 _____

2 _____

Evaluating the results

When you write your conclusion, you may notice the results do not form a pattern.

In your evaluation, you can write about which set of readings you think you should repeat.

If you repeated your readings and found the average, you can say your results are reliable.

SATs practice

Josh investigated dissolving jelly. He wants to know if the temperature of water affects how fast the jelly dissolves.

temperature of water in °C	time taken for jelly to dissolve in minutes			average time for jelly to dissolve in minutes
	Set 1	Set 2	Set 3	
4	30	38	35	34
20	22	21	24	22
40	10	32	9	17
60	2	1	2	1.6

LEVEL 3 Which factor did Josh measure to get the results for his investigation? Tick the correct box.

time taken for jelly ☐   amount of jelly used ☐
to dissolve

amount of water used ☐   time taken to heat up the water ☐

LEVEL 4 Josh thinks he wrote down one set of results incorrectly. Which set of results has an incorrect reading? Circle the set.

(Set 1   Set 2   Set 3)

At which temperature is the incorrect reading? _____°C

LEVEL 5 Josh is writing about these results in his evaluation. Suggest two things Josh could write about in his evaluation.

1 _____

2 _____

Notes